Praise for *The Stake*

In these times of global crisis and opportunity, we need leaders who will stand firmly in their purpose and values, who know how to create intimate and resilient relationships with others, and most importantly who recognize that leadership has nothing to do with control or domination. This brilliant book takes us on a journey of discovering how to do just that. Populated with inspiring stories and potent examples, authors Henry Kimsey-House and David Skibbins take the reader through a process of discovery with a group of people who are uncovering their own leadership abilities and learning the power of taking a stand. I heartily recommend this fascinating and powerful book to everyone everywhere. Its message is critical and a vital contribution to our time.

Lynne Twist
Author, *The Soul of Money*; Founder, Soul of Money Institute;
and Cofounder, The Pachamama Alliance

The Stake: The Making of Leaders *reveals how knowing our life purpose enables us all to keep moving forward into the unknown, driven by the deep curiosity of the impact we can have on ourselves and the whole environment in which we lead. Understanding that the power to lead comes from within us and how we can impact both the people and the space around us is a compelling reason to keep exploring on our personal leadership journeys.*

Ian Stephenson
Vice President, Organization Effectiveness, Cargill

The Co-Active Leadership model is a brilliant work of vision and passion. I had the good fortune and privilege of learning it from Henry and Karen Kimsey-House as they co-led my CTI leadership program. I experienced Henry as the gentlest and wisest "bigge   *life" person I have ever met. Over the subsequent years of work*   *come my model for purity and integrity of visio*   *constant temptations of convenient cor*   *realized that what I had experien*

D1446197

manifestation of the Co-Active Leadership model in action. The uncompromising steadiness I had experienced in him came from his being tethered to his passionate stake for the world and his contribution to it. He had helped to create the model, and was now being guided by the model. And it showed.

It is always challenging to translate something bigger than life, such as Henry and the magic of Co-Active Leadership, through mere words. The two vehicles that tend to transcend such limitations are stories and poetry. Henry and David have artfully used both to accomplish that near impossible task. This book is a must-read for anyone wishing to awaken to the spectacular power of their dormant leadership.

Shirzad Chamine

New York Times bestselling author of Positive Intelligence

THE STAKE

THE MAKING OF LEADERS

HENRY KIMSEY-HOUSE

&

DAVID SKIBBINS

co-active
press

2013

The Stake: The Making of Leaders

Copyright © 2013 by Henry Kimsey-House & David Skibbins

For permission requests, please address:
Co-Active Press
4000 Civic Center Drive, 5th floor
San Rafael, CA 94903

Trademarks referenced in this book are the property of their respective owners.

First published 2013

Printed and bound in the United States of America.

ISBN: 978-1-940159-00-3

Library of Congress Control Number: 2013941362

*This book is dedicated to Karen and Laura
and to the leader in each and every one of us.*

Contents

Introduction

Leadership is not so much about technique and methods as it is about opening the heart. Leadership is about inspiration—of oneself and of others. Great leadership is about human experiences, not processes. Leadership is not a formula or a program, it is a human activity that comes from the heart and considers the hearts of others. It is an attitude, not a routine.

Lance Secretan

William Shakespeare wrote, "Some are born great, some achieve greatness and some have greatness thrust upon them." That is equally applicable to leadership. Sooner or later we all have leadership thrust upon us. It may be an employee, a team, a family, or an organization in your community. Eventually, everyone gets called upon to stand up and say, "Follow me." If it is your turn to step up and lead, then lead with fire.

Rudy Giuliani was mayor of New York City when terrorists flew airliners into the World Trade Center. He was already there on the street when the second plane hit. For most of the next twenty-four hours, he was at the site, or touring hospitals, comforting families, or broadcasting to reassure his constituency and all Americans. We needed his intensity when he said, "Tomorrow New York is going to be here. And we're going to rebuild, and we're going to be stronger than we were before. I want the people of New York to be an example to the rest of the country, and the rest of the world, that terrorism can't stop us."

That was passionate leadership.

This book is about how you can become a passionate leader. We titled this book *The Stake* because we believe that a leader with a passionate Stake is unstoppable. Your Stake, as a leader, is a concise, compelling statement of why you are leading the people you lead. It expresses your willingness to put everything on the line, your vision, and your passionate commitment to an outcome.

You drive a stake into the ground, and it holds up whatever you attach to it. As a leader, you are tethered to your Leader's Stake so that it becomes the orientation point for everything you do. If you begin to stray away from the Stake, the Stake itself is so compelling and is planted so firmly that it pulls you back on course. Mayor Giuliani had a Stake: "New York City and America are stronger and greater than a handful of criminal terrorists!" The authors of this book have a Stake: "This book will inspire leaders to create change and transformation in the world."

What does it take to lead with fire? Leaders need to know what they are passionate about. They need to know what strengths and skills they can call upon to move that passion into reality. They need to have a full range of expression, plus highly attuned emotional intelligence, to be able to express their passion in a compelling way. Above all, they need to have a really strong urge to make the world a better place because they have taken charge.

How can one train this kind of leadership? This question inspired Henry Kimsey-House to create the Co-Active Leadership Program. Over the past two decades, Henry Kimsey-House's international leadership training organization, the Coaches Training Institute, co-created with Laura Whitworth and Karen Kimsey-House, has trained more than 1,800 graduates from all over the world to lead from their passion, using the leadership model that he helped create. In the Co-Active Leadership Program, a group of twenty-five to thirty participants go through intensive year-long training as a cohort group called a "tribe." You, the reader, are about to experience a cutting-edge approach to developing innovative, passionate leadership in business, governments, nonprofit organizations, and communities.

The Co-Active Leadership Program focuses on teaching skills in five areas:

Strength: Passionate leaders need to act with authenticity and marshal their personal powers and strengths in the service of their Stake.

Connection: Leaders need to create connection and intimacy in many arenas—one on one; with small groups, teams, companies, and communities; and even with nations.

Awareness: To create connection and intimacy, leaders need to know how to read and manage the emotional energy of individuals and groups.

Responsibility: Leaders need to know how to be aware of, and take responsibility for, their impact on the individuals, teams, companies, and organizations that they lead. They need to know how to lead from their purpose and mission, instead of from their ego.

Service: Finally, leaders need to be willing to serve—life, humanity, the people they lead, and themselves, in that order.

The characters you will meet in this book are entirely fictional, with the exception of three real graduates of the Leadership Program: three people who went out and changed the world. Victoria Bently works with displaced African women; Ted van der Put works in corporate Europe to promote sustainability in the face of climate change; and Celeste Schenck is leading a major world university to transform its teaching model. Through their stories, you will see how Co-Active Leadership can make an impact in the real world.

The poet and political activist Muriel Rukeyser wrote, "The universe is made of stories, not of atoms." So we're telling a story to explain the concepts of leadership presented in this book. Although it's a work of fiction, it is also an accurate portrayal of the impact of this course, based on the actual experiences we have observed over years of conducting these programs.

Weaving content about leadership into an ongoing narrative makes for enjoyable reading. Hopefully, it also puts some flesh on the bones of the core concepts of Co-Active Leadership. But for those who want "just the facts, ma'am," and for those who want a quick review after they have read the book, we include a summary of these concepts after the story of each retreat.

While we sought to capture the intent of the exercises that participants experience during the Co-Active Leadership Program, we have intentionally changed the exercises in this book so that, should you decide to take the leadership course, you will be as surprised as anyone who hasn't read the book.

We will be referring to the Co-Active Leadership model often in this book, so we are including a map of that model in the introduction, so that you can flip back and refer to it whenever you want to. It looks like this:

The Co-Active® Leadership Model

So, light the fire, heat up some cocoa, wrap a blanket around you, and settle in for an absorbing and engaging journey of discovery.

"Once upon a time . . . "

Chapter One

On the Road

Never doubt that a small group of thoughtful, committed citizens can change the world. Indeed, it is the only thing that ever has.

Margaret Mead

Stella Mancusi was thoroughly sick of the snow and of the bitter northwest winds that gusted relentlessly in over the lake. The hard-frozen surface crackled as her boots broke through and sank into the dry, squeaky powder underneath. The icy claws of the northern Wisconsin winter pierced deep. You could walk over a mile from shore on the frozen bays of Lake Superior, if you were stupid enough. Inland, on the Bad River Band Reservation, everything and everyone had retreated into some form of hibernation.

She wasn't built for this weather—she was too muscular and too tall. She needed a lot more padding. Stella kicked the snow off her boots and stepped up into her Jeep. It turned over after only a few tries—a good sign. She threw her bags on the back seat, and she was ready to roll. In a few hours, she would be out of this godforsaken freezer! She said a brief prayer to protect her grandmother, her nieces and nephews, and all living beings on the reservation. As she turned onto Highway 2 to begin the 150-mile trek to the Minneapolis–St. Paul airport and her flight to California, she began to sing. She was off to lead a new leadership group in sunny California. She really loved this work!

Zeke Aaronson sat on the lid of his Samsonite suitcase, trying to push it down far enough to close the latch. This time he'd really over-packed! However, his 285 pounds should be more than enough to do the job. *Yet another advantage to being as big as a bear*, he thought. Then he smiled, thinking of the eight-foot-tall, nine-hundred-pound black bear he had surprised when fishing the North Thompson River in the Monashee Mountains of British Columbia. *Okay, a small bear.*

He was heading off to lead another CTI Leadership Program. It was opening week of this series of four weeklong retreats that spread out over almost a full year. He felt a fierce flame of joy. Lives were about to be changed, and he got to be one of the catalysts.

That was okay! And, for a couple of reasons, he was also dreading it a little. For one, his partner, Jason, wanted him to go on a trip to Africa, and this leadership group schedule was going to make that pretty difficult. For another, he remembered that he had led one of these retreats two years ago with Stella Mancusi, the same co-leader he had this time. Last time, they hadn't clicked. Oh, they'd gotten through it, and the participants had had a great experience. But some of the after-hours discussions had been more stressful than he was used to with other co-leaders. He and Stella hadn't meshed in the way he had expected and wanted, and he had been concerned that the course participants hadn't had the duality of leadership experience that he wanted them to have.

Well, what the hell. People change. He knew that he had changed a bunch in the past two years. Maybe Jason would mellow out. Maybe Stella would warm up. And no matter what, he loved this work. It was going to be great. Just a little more effort, and then came that satisfying Samsonite *click*.

Phil Serrito longed just to hire a hit man to take care of that Burbank manager. No, maybe he should just do it himself. That would be so much more rewarding. Bill Sykes was going to drive him to justifiable homicide. Phil slammed his heavy-duty, steel-backed, IBM keyboard down hard on his vintage brushed-steel desk. Then he checked. No scratches. Good! He turned off his computer and ran his finger through his crew cut.

He opened the second drawer on the right and brought out his Nabisco version of Valium. He carefully twisted off the tops of two Oreos, tossed them into his wastepaper basket, and pasted the two open cookies together. A habit from his youth, it soothed him. Being careful not to get crumbs on his desk, he bit gently into this treat.

Why was he doing this damn leadership retreat? He'd already taken a class in leadership. He knew all about adapting his leadership style to the context, harnessing intrinsic motivation, zero-sum games, and creating learning environments. Of course, none of that stuff worked with his rebel manager in Southern California. How much longer was this war going to go on? At least he would have one blissful week away from email.

Two Oreos a day was all he allowed himself, so he chewed slowly in order to enjoy them. And they did give him some peace. These were the last ones he would have for a week. It was unlikely that the retreat center where he was going would carry Oreos. And he wasn't about to risk getting crumbs all over his suitcase if he tried to bring his own. Anticipating the self-imposed abstinence made each bite all the more precious.

Why do *you* have to go away to learn how to be a leader?"

"It can't hurt," she answered.

Isabel Lopez didn't trust the motivation behind her executive assistant's question. She knew he had many complaints that he never shared with her but spewed out to others in her division. Some of her direct reports had already been dropping hints in her direction that he wasn't exactly loyal to her. And she had no illusions about her own leadership style. Okay, she got things done, and if she left a few bruised egos in her wake from time to time, she didn't mind that. But three months ago, she had unexpectedly lost a trusted coordinator, a woman she had thought was a friend. When Denise left, she told Isabel that the chief reason she couldn't stand working there any longer was Isabel's overbearing attitude, her shrieking, and her tendency to micromanage everyone around her.

At that point, Isabel had known she might need a little more leadership training. She hadn't wanted a whole year of it, but a board member whom she trusted had suggested she seriously consider this program. It actually hurt her pride to discover that John felt that she needed help.

She cleaned off the top of her desk, filing everything she didn't just toss out. She wasn't planning on coming back to a mess. When she could see nothing but mahogany, she was ready to leave. It was time to go home to pack. She grabbed her Mackage cashmere coat and slammed her office door as she left.

The numbers on the cardio display were too low. He really needed to pick up the pace. His trainer wasn't going to be happy. Allen Bowers pushed the button to crank up the elevation on the treadmill. He was already dripping sweat. Not that it did any good. He couldn't lose those extra thirty pounds to save his life.

One week free from this torture! He had already checked—the retreat center had no exercise equipment. Thank God! Then Allen smiled. His parishioners in his old congregation wouldn't have thought this was a very appropriate prayer for their minister. But these days he was in administration, so none of them would ever know or care.

He was so ready for something new—life felt so claustrophobic. It had taken a month to convince his superior that this program would ultimately serve the church. Finally, he had the green light. Probably they were just sick of his polite nagging. But it had been years since he had done something completely outside the church and just for himself. He could hardly wait!

He looked up. Finally—thirty minutes. Now he could escape with a clear conscience, and maybe grab some Häagen-Dazs on the way home.

Olivia Stimson didn't feel she was having much of an impact in the classroom anymore, and the leadership course seemed like her last opportunity to make something of her faltering career in teaching. She'd arranged for a substitute to cover her classes and wondered if her students would notice the change.

There was one last detail to take care of. "Who's going to take care of you?" she asked, as she sat in the afternoon sun, gently stroking her cat, Magritte. The gaunt old tabby stretched to acknowledge her concern and then coiled himself in a yellow spot of light. That spot soon faded. Olivia looked out her arched window toward the hills. A gray cloud was lumbering in to block the sun.

She was going to have to break down and ask her sister—her beautiful, successful, and always-generous sister. Molly would say, "Of course. I will come over three times a day and even spend some evenings watching TV so Magritte won't get too lonely."

And Olivia would add one more item to the lengthy list of reasons why her sister was so much better a person than she was.

She whispered to her cat, "I hope that psychic was right and that reincarnation is true, Mags. She told me that Molly was my Inquisitioner in medieval Spain and I suffered horribly under her heartless ministrations. This lifetime is one of reparation, right? That must be true, because the only other possible alternative is that I am a selfish bitch who continuously exploits the kindness of her co-dependent sister. Now, that can't possibly be true, right, honey?"

Magritte did not deign to reply.

Emily Ross pushed the button that ended her last client call of the day. She finished writing down the coaching homework she had given him, then she closed his file and put it into the beige HON file cabinet next to her desk. She stood up, stretched, and made the ten-step commute from her office down the hallway to her kitchen.

She looked around her one-bedroom bungalow. It was the first house she had ever owned all by herself, and she loved it. Every curtain, every Oriental rug, every painting, the overstuffed couch and the Second Empire side table—all of the things she had bought because each one spoke to her. A warm smile spread across her face as she simply stood there, soaking in the beauty she had created all around her.

This was her last supper. Her last chance to enjoy her own cooking for a week. A friend who had already taken Leadership told her that the food would be very healthy and natural at the retreat center. As Emily added the room-temperature heavy cream to her pasta carbonara, she thought, *At least I might lose some weight while I'm away.* She could survive having to eat Granola for a week. Somehow.

Chapter Two

Creating from Self

Enthusiasm is one of the most powerful engines of success. When you do a thing, do it with all your might. Put your whole soul into it. Stamp it with your own personality. Be active, be energetic and faithful, and you will accomplish your object. Nothing great was ever achieved without enthusiasm.

Ralph Waldo Emerson

"**The sun** is going nova soon. Humanity has time to design and build just one spaceship. You are the finalists in an Earth-wide contest to see who gets to be on that ship. There are only fifteen seats left. You must present your case to the group. Justify why you should be aboard. The group will vote who will go, while the rest of you will stay on this doomed planet. Begin."

It was late afternoon. The introductions were over, and this was the first exercise of the first retreat. Zeke was standing in front of twenty-three strangers in a large, rustic event room, all sitting on chairs in a semicircle, facing the two leaders at the front. Zeke was very large, both physically and energetically, and rather intimidating. His voice was deep, and he spoke slowly as he announced the exercise.

Oh, damn! Emily thought to herself. She resented this stupid *Star Wars* exercise. What the hell was she doing at a leadership training retreat, anyway? This psychodrama stuff was so old-school! She had been through this kind of training twenty-odd years ago, while studying group therapy at her university. Even back then she'd thought it was a big waste of time, and her opinion hadn't changed any since then. *I don't need this crap to be a better executive coach. Why am I here?*

As the participants went on and on about how they were going to do this exercise, Emily tuned out. In her mind, she was tracing back to the origin of her apparently poor decision to join this leadership training. It had begun in a time of new beginnings, when her second daughter, Francine, had left for college—new opportunities for growth and intimacy with her husband, and for her own flowering as a professional.

She'd decided to create some changes in her life—empty nest and all that. After twenty years as a therapist, things were getting stale. Too many wounded souls. Time for a change—maybe even a new direction—so she'd started training to become an executive coach. Working with healthy people turned out to be a lot more fun.

And then everything had collapsed. It was the lilacs. Sitting in the Leadership event room, she suddenly smelled lilacs. She looked around. Not a purple bloom in sight. Heck, this was California, hundreds of miles from the nearest fragrant lilac bush.

Then she remembered the rest of it. The day everything fell apart. Lilacs had been in full bloom, draping over the railing of their Connecticut colonial. She remembered the morning when she and Mike had sat on their sun porch, sipping their English Breakfast tea and watching the sun begin to warm their front yard. Mike had set his cup down and looked at her. Deep sigh. Then, "Emily, I'm moving out."

That eviscerating memory still lurked inside her, waiting for the most inopportune moments to re-infect her. Lilacs, and the end of life as she had known it for twenty-three years.

When her husband left her to marry someone fourteen years younger, Emily knew she had two choices: to rot or to run. Either she could sit in an empty house, watching reruns into the early mornings and ruminating over how many years of her life she had wasted taking care of that jerk's needs, or she could jump into a new adventure and explore a bittersweet, unpredictable new life. And so she made her choice. She sold her house within a month, closed her therapy practice, and headed across the country to California. For a while she'd thought seriously about heading in the opposite direction, to northern Italy, but that was a tiny bit more ambitious than she could handle at the time.

Coaching sessions with her clients were done primarily on the telephone, so she could actually live anywhere she wanted to. She found herself a tiny but charming condo to live in temporarily. Unfortunately, while she enjoyed the coaching, she missed doing therapy, so when a part-time clinical position in a local women's shelter opened up, she grabbed it. On a friend's recommendation, she decided to use some of this extra income to try CTI's Leadership Program. It was offered by the same company that had provided her coaching training. She was hoping that it would help her find a way to ground herself in this new world she had plunged into.

Right now she hated her friend who had told her that the CTI Leadership Program would change her life. For sure, her life needed some changing. But this group-fantasy exercise made it clear that her choice to go to CTI Leadership was turning out to be a terribly expensive mistake.

"This is brainwashing!" she muttered under her breath. At this very moment, sitting in this event room, she regretted not finding a sun-tanned lover and learning Italian.

The first volunteer stood up in front of the group to speak. She was a trim, middle-aged Latina woman wearing very high-end business-casual clothing—a little overdressed for this crowd. She was Emily's roommate for this retreat, but they hadn't talked to each other much before this opening meeting.

"I'm Isabel Lopez, and I lead the fund-raising program for the Shelter for the Disabled Foundation. Thanks to our efforts, five thousand disabled people were taken off the streets last year. I will bring these humanistic values . . . "

As the rather shrill female voice went on, Emily began to worry about what she was going to say. What she wanted to say was, Hi, I'm Emily Ross. I'm staying here on Earth. Have a nice trip, and hand me the barbecue sauce. My life is turning into ashes anyway. An inferno is beginning to look like a step up. At least I won't have to endure these stupid simulations.

She realized that this line of thought was probably a little too dark for this group. Gallows humor—not a good sign. Her self-esteem had been in the crapper since the divorce. She hated to admit it to herself, but she needed more than a few leadership skills here—she needed a reason to keep going!

When it was her turn to speak, she stood in front of the group and looked around the room. She wasn't the only one having a hard time. A cute but rather chubby minister named Allen Bowers and a nervous, breathless younger woman named Olivia had already volunteered to stay behind. She definitely didn't want to join this voluntary victim group!

She decided to play the game. Hey, she knew how to put on a mask. No one in her life really knew how bad she felt inside. This was just another chance to practice those masquerade skills.

"I'm older than the rest of you, so I know I'm not a good candidate to survive this vote. I mean, the last person up here, Loretta, is pregnant. Heck, I would vote for her to live instead of me. But I've been a psychotherapist for decades, and considering that the folks on this trip will be grieving the loss of their whole planet, I think they're going to need a lot of mental and emotional support." She knew it was lame, but it was the best she could do.

Emily was surprisingly relieved to find that when the vote was taken, she wasn't among the loser group to be incinerated. What she had said must have been good enough. *It sure wasn't my stunning good looks*, she thought.

Then the leaders opened the discussion and invited everyone to give each other honest feedback. The feedback she received from the others in the group was pretty hard for her to hear. She felt as if she had conned the people who voted for her. Some of the group bought into her plea and appreciated her commitment to supporting the survivors. Oh well—what the hell. At least she hadn't gotten left behind.

But some of them saw through her shabby mask. They told her that she came across as flat and only half-alive. That was a fair comment. Several others said that they thought her cold and uninterested. Also true.

Then Stella Mancusi spoke to her. She was the female co-leader of the program, a tall, athletic, brown-eyed woman with long black hair that had a striking streak of white running through it. She looked close to Emily's age, maybe a little younger, and wore a chunky turquoise necklace.

"You're living a small, gray life," she said. That nailed it. But it didn't help Emily get out of her fog.

When Zeke stood up, he gave her the most confusing feedback of all. He looked down at her. "It's as though you were stuck in the worst aspects of Level One Awareness down there." When she looked at him blankly, he explained.

"Level One Awareness is when we focus on our inner thoughts and feelings. It's the first of three different levels of awareness. Level Two is when we focus all our attention on the person right in front of us. To get to Level Three Awareness, we soften our focus and become aware of everything around us. Each level has its usefulness and its traps. Right now, I want us to look at Level One: focus on self.

"Level One Awareness is a total focus of our attention on our internal monologue. It's an awareness of all the different conversations going on inside us—mostly conversations about ourselves, but sometimes about other people. It's the fascinated concentration on all our inner judgments, opinions, arguments, worries, lectures, daydreams, 3:00 AM monologues, on and on, ad infinitum."

As Zeke sat down, Stella added, "Mind you, Level One Awareness is not always a bad place to be. In its best aspects, it can be an inspiring place. It includes all of the powerful thoughts, beliefs, opinions, attitudes, values, purpose, and identity that make up our true selves. In its best form, we call this face of Level One Awareness 'the Grounded Self.'"

Zeke laughed. "But, Emily, you were definitely not your Grounded Self up there at the front of the room. Unfortunately, Level One Awareness can also include all of our self-destructive, limiting, negative chatter. The evil twin of the Grounded Self is the Destructive Self. The Destructive Self includes the judgments, betrayals of self, justifications, excuses, and old stories that we tell ourselves over and over again. These negative diatribes seek to attack, limit, and constrict us. Those were the voices that made you look weak and whiny up there. It was your Destructive Self who was telling you that you weren't worth saving."

Stella stepped in again. "Oh, and by the way, you are definitely not the only person in this room struggling with that kind of negative conversation." There was sympathetic laughter from some of the group.

As a psychotherapist, Emily knew all this, but she said nothing and just waited. What else were they driving at?

Stella walked over to the flip chart and wrote *Grounded Self* and *Destructive Self*. Then she turned to Emily. "In order for you—and everyone else in this room—to move into powerful leadership, you must be able to distinguish these two different voices within yourself. Our work on ourselves as leaders is to learn to feed the Grounded Self and to starve the Destructive Self. It's hard work! The Destructive Self habitually gets the most of our attention and can dominate the way we see others and the world around us.

"So one of the first things you will need to focus on in your life as a leader is how to strengthen the Grounded Self and how to expose the Destructive Self. Do this well, and the Grounded Self can go to work growing, creating, and providing powerful leadership. It can avoid the trap set by the Destructive Self, by refocusing your awareness away from all of those self-destructive conversations that are such a recurring nightmare for so many of us."

Then Zeke looked hard at Emily, almost as if he could hear the cacophony of judgments that were going on inside her head about what he was telling her. He said, "It's very important for any leader to clean up their Level One Awareness conversations, and to challenge the power that their Destructive Self has over them. I know you are a trained psychotherapist, so you already know how critical this work is. A lot of psychotherapy is about understanding where and how these negative messages originate. Healing those wounds that feed the Destructive Self is a lifelong path that every leader must travel. Many books, workshops, and spiritual disciplines focus on that process.

"Emily, your background as a therapist should put you in good stead in doing this work, and I am sure you have done some of it already. That work is essential for you to be able to step confidently into leadership. It's also the ongoing spiritual work of being human. However, it's not the focus of this week's work."

Good, she thought. *I didn't sign up for a group psychotherapy marathon. Maybe now you'll get to the point!*

Zeke went over to the flip chart, crossed out the words *Destructive Self*, and underlined *Grounded Self*.

"In this program, we come at the situation a little differently. We don't spend a lot of time analyzing your Destructive Self. We work primarily on strengthening your Grounded Self, so that you can lead powerfully, with clarity and purpose. And, as you can see from this last exercise, that is going to be challenging for all of you. I didn't see any Grounded Selves up there when you were talking."

Zeke's words smarted. Emily knew he was right on target. While she had been up there speaking, her inner judge and critic had definitely taken over. Some part of her didn't think she was worth a seat on that rocket. Her focus had been on hating herself and hating the exercise. She realized that she had been practically holding her breath the whole time Stella and Zeke were talking to her. She had frozen because they were telling her things she knew but didn't want to acknowledge.

At least she could take solace in the fact that she hadn't been voted to be fried by the sun; that honor had gone to eight others. Olivia, the slight woman whose voice was so soft it was hard to hear her, had burst into tears when she received feedback on how she had betrayed herself by volunteering to die. Perhaps the most pathetic person to be burned up by the sun was Allen, the minister. He'd pleaded eloquently to be a martyr for the group. Stella had confronted him directly on selling his life short for the sake of other people's needs.

Living for others. Ouch! Stella's work on Allen hit a little too close to home for Emily.

The session was finally over. Instead of unpacking or getting ready for dinner, Emily needed to walk. She didn't want to be social right now. The retreat center was perched on the side of a ridge overlooking the Pacific Ocean. Looking in one direction, she could see all the way to the horizon. The other side of the center was nestled into a grove of redwood trees.

She followed a narrow trail into the woods that finally led to a small stream. She stopped and sat down by the brook, just staring at the gentle riffle. She felt soothed by the soft slosh of the rivulets as they slid over tiny waterfalls.

She needed soothing right now. She could feel the emotional black hole she was in. Making that bold "westward ho" move to California hadn't been enough to pull her out of her pit, at least not yet. Maybe nothing was going to work.

She sat there, feeling numb and alone. She wondered if maybe she shouldn't just get in her car right now and crawl back to her new house, a house that still didn't feel like a home. Instead, she stood up, brushed off her pants, and headed back to the center.

Dinner was uncomfortable for her. Emily had lost her capacity to indulge in small talk and chatter. Too many years working with seriously disturbed therapy clients. And she just didn't care about the weather.

She'd much rather devote her full attention to the excellent fillet of sole in front of her, but she was too polite to say so. She put in the effort and tried to chat, burying her resentment at not getting to enjoy her food in peace, but she was the first one out of the dining room after the meal was over.

As she lay in bed, sleepless and staring into the darkness, she realized that she couldn't remember a single word that any of her dinner companions had said. All she could think of was that coming to this leadership program had been a great big mistake!

Next morning, the opening exercise was for each member of the group to answer the question, "What were you born to do in this lifetime?" Emily had already asked herself that question more than once in the past several months and had come up with nothing. For twenty-three years, she had thought the meaning of her life was to love and to serve. She had done it well, loving and serving her clients and her family. Then that had all gone bust.

Okay, not completely bust. Her daughter was a huge gift to her life and had been a great support through the breakup. But Emily certainly didn't want to burden her daughter, or anyone else, with the messy depression inside her, or the feeling of emptiness in her life. She wasn't ready to answer that question. She began listening more closely to what the leaders were saying.

Zeke was speaking. "Being able to answer that question about your life's purpose in a heartfelt manner is crucial for any leader. So the next exercise is very simple, but that doesn't mean that you'll find it easy. You're going to spend an hour in solitude and silence to write in your journal. At the end of the hour, and still in silence, come back to the event room. One by one, you'll declare your Life Purpose to the group. The silence and the exercise start now. We will see you back here in an hour."

For Emily, this was a whole new level of hell. She walked away from the event room, going deep into the redwoods along the path she had explored the day before. She needed to walk, so she went far beyond the stream where she had rested before. She was breathing heavily as she climbed an endless uphill stretch in the path. Suddenly, she turned a corner and found herself looking out at a robin's-egg-blue sky, above the endless ocean. Far below her, she saw plumes of white spray where waves broke against the rocky shore.

She sat down on a flat rock and opened her journal. She was not going to be able to escape this emptiness. Maybe there was no purpose to her life. But if that were the case, then at least she would face it right now.

But, once back in the event room, Emily found herself changing again. There was no way she was going to go first. As she looked around the room, she saw at least a few other people appearing to be as wrecked as she felt. At least she wasn't alone.

Allen stood up first, tucked his work shirt into his jeans, and walked to the front of the room. "I can't get the image of the defrocked minister in Tennessee Williams's *The Night of the Iguana* out of my head. He had just about lost his faith as he sank into a deep well of self-hatred. But I am not that badly off." He smiled. "My Life Purpose is to see the face of God in every person in front of me as long as I breathe."

Olivia followed him. Her small hands were trembling, and for a long time she just stood silently in front of everyone. Finally, she said, very softly, "Today is the seventh anniversary of the death of my father. He was a funny, wonderful man, and he loved me very much. I was at his bedside at the hospital when he died. I hate people calling it 'passing beyond' or 'making the transition.' He's dead, and my world isn't really quite as bright without him. But I know I have only a limited number of breaths myself before I take my last one. So my Life Purpose is to live every single breath with my arms wide open."

Isabel stood up next and walked gracefully to the front. Her presence, and her elegant suit, commanded everyone's attention. "My sister Josephina gave birth last week to a beautiful boy named Ramon. I held him just a few moments after he came out of her womb. His eyes were open and so deep. My Life Purpose is to do everything I can to see that the world he grows up in, and the planet he grows up on, is healthier, cleaner, and more loving than the world I grew up in."

Phil, a muscular guy with a short crew cut, strode up to the front. He had introduced himself as an executive, but right now he looked more like a jock. "My Life Purpose is all wrapped up with my job. I love my work. Almost every morning I wake up and I can't wait to get to the office. I'm responsible for the seventy-five people who report to me. Sure, they drive me crazy sometimes. One of them is doing a bang-up job at that right now. But that's part of the challenge. So my Life Purpose is to show up as a leader in such a powerful way that every one of them experiences their work as fulfilling, challenging, and fun. I want them to love what we do together just as much as I do."

Emily knew it was now her moment to speak. She didn't remember standing up or walking around the circle of chairs, but suddenly, there she was, facing the group. She saw the open interest in their eyes and took a deep breath.

"Okay, here goes. I was going to come up here and tell you I had failed and hadn't found any big, compelling Life Purpose. See, my husband of twenty-three years left me for a sweet young thing. Or at least she was a lot younger than I am. And my heart closed. But just now, listening to Olivia, I realized that I'm starting to get over that. I'm tired of walking around with a half-open heart. I've been hurt. It was a big deal when it happened. But that was then, and this is now. So my Life Purpose is to love anyway. No matter what happens."

At the end of the exercise, Zeke and Stella returned to the front of the room. "Great job, everyone," said Stella. "You took your first shot at defining a reason to lead. Hopefully, each of you will be tweaking, modifying, changing, and evolving your Life Purpose Statement for the rest of your life, as you grow and change. Discovering your purpose, your work this lifetime, helps you craft your Leaders' Stakes. So now let's find out exactly what I mean by that term, *Leader's Stake*."

She pointed to a poster of the Co-Active Leadership Model.

"Okay, the first thing I want to say about this model is, don't be intimidated by it! By the end of this program, it will make sense. Right now—"

Zeke broke in, "It better make sense by the end of the program! Or we blew it."

Stella went on, "Right, but for now, just hang out with it without trying to understand it all right away. The Co-Active Leadership Model is a circle of the things a leader pays attention to, things that constantly circle around this star-shaped thing in the center, this thing we call the Leader's Stake. We'll talk about each of the model's elements on the outside ring over time, but today let's just start in the center. So, what is a Leader's Stake?"

Zeke said, "Let's start by talking about what a Stake isn't. It's not a goal, like 'make more profits,' 'increase sales,' or 'improve productivity.' None of these is a focal point for a Leader. Hey, they are important, no question about it. But they are the goals of managers. Goals are practical milestones toward a specific end. Nothing wrong with goals; they are very useful. It's just that goals don't inspire. Goals just clearly identify steps along the path. They don't tell you why you got on the path in the first place.

The Co-Active® Leadership Model

"This morning you were creating compelling statements about the passions that motivate you. At CTI, we call these Life Purpose Statements. Your Life Purpose is the meaning, purpose, and reason why you were born on this planet at this time, and it defines the work you were meant to do. 'I am here to make a better world for my nephew.' 'I lead to inspire.' 'I want to see the face of God.' These Life Purpose Statements define your actions.

"Imagine your life is a river and your Life Purpose is the current, pulling you along and moving you onward through your life. There will be all sorts of speed changes in this current as it moves over rapids, waterfalls, and eddies. There may be pools of stillness, yet the current is always there, guiding you down the river of your life.

"Your Life Purpose influences any Stake you choose to set, and any Stake you set is wrapped around the unshakeable core of your Life Purpose. Life Purpose is what helps you choose the Stakes that you do set.

"A Leader's Stake is planted whenever a leader takes responsibility for an event that calls for their leadership. It's through these Stakes that your Life Purpose manifests itself in concrete projects that lead to concrete change. A leader is tethered to their Leader's Stake so that it becomes the orientation point for everything that occurs around the event. Whenever the leader begins to stray away from their Stake, the Stake itself is so compelling, and so firmly planted, that it pulls the leader back on course."

Stella stepped in. "Another metaphor to describe it is that the Leader's Stake is the lens that the leader looks through at everything concerning the event. It orients your vision. For example, your Life Purpose Statement might be: 'With love and authenticity, I inspire people to become more alive!' That purpose will inform every Stake you set. Suppose you and another person are designing a workshop. The two of you may co-create a Stake that you share for that particular workshop. Let's say the workshop's name is 'The Creative Moment.' Your Stake could be something like, 'Intimacy and connection open the door to vast creativity!' You might easily align to that Stake because it's so in focus with your Life Purpose."

Zeke stood up and pointed to the various elements on the Co-Active Leadership Model, charting a journey around the circle. "Let's take a look at all the phases of leadership on the circumference of this Leadership Model—that orbit around your Leader Stake. I'm going to start at the top of this chart. In any leadership moment, you are attuned to the needs of the group, the needs of the environment, your own needs, and the needs of the Leader's Stake. This is what we call Level Three Awareness.

"Now let's go clockwise around the circle. You stay attuned to this awareness until you get an urge to act to meet one or more of those needs. Then you make the choice to act.

"You take action with all of your being, not tentatively, not holding back—making a powerful impact on your world. We call this Full Permission. But at the same time, you stay present and attuned, watching the impact of your actions, taking full responsibility for the impact you are making on those you lead.

"Then, using Level Three Awareness, you stay present for the results of your action and then wait for the next urge to hit you. When your Stake is clear, you will find yourself moving around and around this model in a continual motion, and you will be in the full flow of leadership."

The whole model sounded pretty academic to Emily, and not very useful. But the concept of the Stake began to make some sense when Stella added her perspective.

"Okay, I'm sensing folks are getting a little lost," she said. "Let's get back to the Stake. Just get this: Remember that a Stake is not a goal or an outcome. Goals *serve* the Stake. For a leader, however, the goals that are set must be true to the Leader's Stake.

"The Stake is the leader's orientation, and it may also become the orientation of those he or she leads. Stakes are the glasses leaders see the world through. They bring into focus what is needed to achieve a world aligned with the Stake. For instance, right now, Zeke and I may have a goal called 'All of you sitting out there shall get a preliminary understanding of this circular leadership model.' But that goal is a small part of the larger Stake we have about experiential learning. That Stake is 'Experiential learning is magic, wonder, awe, love, and mastery all rolled into one.'"

Zeke continued, "Leadership begins as an inside job. The discovery of your calling to lead is a profoundly private, intimate, personal experience. A voice deep within says something like, *This must come to pass!* or, *This must stop!* or, *Not on my watch!* or, *This is for my family (or my team or my community or my people or my nation).* Leadership arises from an injunction, an inner knowing, a determination that impels you to take action. This internal commandment, applied to a specific project or event, is what we call a Leader's Stake.

"You may be wondering why we use the word *Stake.* It has nothing to do with Buffy the Vampire Slayer. Well, maybe a little bit. We do want to drive a stake into the heart of the Destructive Self.

"A stake is a pointed stick that can hold something up, like a tent, or mark a boundary, like a surveyor's stake. It can also be a sum of money that you put up to play poker or to participate in a business venture. And it can be a tall post, as in being burned at the stake. The way we use the term draws from all three definitions. We are using the definition of *Stake* to mean asserting one's share in an endeavor, defining our territory, and acknowledging our investment in the outcome. We stake our claim, whether it's in the gold fields near Sutter's Mill or in the boardrooms on Wall Street. It is the anchor point from which we can lead.

"But there's more work to be done before we do any more exploring about what a Stake is. We have to start with who is pounding that Stake into the ground. It's not possible to set your Stake just arbitrarily. First off, you must know who you are. Finding out who you are and what you stand for is the genesis of leadership. The leader's connection with his or her fundamental strengths, foundational beliefs, and core principles is central to effective leadership. And that's what this retreat is about."

Isabel stood up and said, "Wait a minute—this is still very confusing. Is the Stake an outcome, or an internal commandment, or a vision statement, or an investment, or a mission, or just a pointed stick? You really haven't made this clear. What are you talking about?"

Zeke laughed. "Good point, Isabel. You know, maybe it's a little of all of the above."

Stella looked at him and then turned to Isabel.

"I understand and appreciate your desire for clarity here. And I wish we could give you the simple, five-word definition that clears everything up. But leadership is more of an art than a science. And this metaphor we are calling the Stake has more to do with poetry than with precision. When you are defining a Stake that you are willing to devote your life energy to, it's like trying to wrap words around a passion so deeply felt that the words can never quite capture its core. You know you are close when your heart says, *Yes, that's what I want to do!* All I can ask you to do right now is to let our definition be a little imprecise, and to keep trying to discover what the concept means to you."

Isabel said, "I'll try" and sat down. But Emily thought she didn't look very satisfied with that answer.

Stella stood up. "Okay, enough of this talk. You have to experience this for yourself. What are you on the planet to accomplish? In the next series of exercises, we are going to help you refine your Life Purpose, the reason why you were put on the planet for this lifetime."

During the next few exercises, Emily had a hard time coming up with anything very compelling to help her strengthen her Life Purpose statement. At times her mind seemed completely blank and shut down, either from sleepiness or from something else. But the phrase *not on my watch* kept coming back. During the silent journal period, she didn't write a thing. Instead she thought back to her best friend, Victoria Bently, who had convinced her to take the leadership course. She recalled the discussion they had had about a month earlier.

Victoria had warned her, "Fasten your seat belt; the CTI leadership course will change your life. It did mine, radically! One Sunday, I remember sitting on the balcony, peacefully drinking my Earl Grey tea, reading my Sunday *Los Angeles Times*, and watching the sun light up the Santa Barbara hills. I started reading a long article about the Congo.

"A woman had been raped by rebels and then disowned by her husband and driven from their village. The husband made her take the children and then got another wife. I couldn't get that damn article out of my mind. But what was I supposed to do? Be the great white savior and go to Africa and rescue these women? Not likely. Or should I just forget it and go to Nordstrom?

"A month later, I was in that damn first leadership retreat. In a ritual of declaration, inside a huge, burned-out redwood stump the size of a room, I said out loud, 'I will go to Africa and help those women.' Everything in my life changed after that moment.

"If you take this course, Emily, you're going to learn a whole lot about your Life Purpose. And there's so much to learn! My Life Purpose created my own Stake, which for me is an organizing thought, the plan that I use to stay focused on my goal when all else around me seems to be falling apart. My Stake keeps me on the path during difficult times. At first it was the organizing principle, that flash of focused commitment that made a general vision so much more specific—the vehicle through which my impulse to action was realized. Later, it became the guiding light, Carl Jung's 'lantern in the darkness.' My Stake continues to define and illuminate the path that I have chosen.

"And sometimes it's my road out of hell. The Congo is such a scary and beautiful land of contrast and contradiction: a country of enormous wealth with no roads, starvation in the midst of bounty, appalling cruelty combined with genuine warmth, as enigmatic today as it was when Stanley sought the source of the Nile. What surprises me most about that country is the people: they are the friendliest, warmest people I have ever met. They smile and shake your hand on the street, just to say hello. The Congolese laugh and joke all the time; they have fun with each other. And their music sets the standard for all Africa: the Congolese rumba may be the best dance music in the world. And yet, unspeakable crimes against women occur every day, and an estimated thirty-eight thousand people, mostly women and children, die every month from starvation, disease, and neglect.

"Thank God I wasn't attached to *how* I was going to help these women! I wanted to start with rape and trauma counseling, but my original ideas were way too ambitious. My first big challenge was getting just two women and their two sewing machines out of the tiny lean-to they called a center and into a better building. When I asked if they would rather have new machines or a new roof, they went for the machines, since sewing is their hope for the future. How they got anything done in the rain and mud, I do not know.

"Here in the States, we just don't get it. Nothing here compares to the situation in the Congo. Even in our worst slums, people have a roof and a cement floor, a homeless shelter or soup kitchen to go to. Not in the Congo. But the women there are very resilient. Despite all that has happened to them, they are enthusiastic and intent on learning how to sew. I am deeply touched by these brave women, and profoundly moved to action. They asked me if I would be their liaison with the West, and I accepted with pleasure.

"When I run into obstacles, like corruption, bureaucratic barriers, or cultural conflicts, I use my Stake to get me back on track and aligned with what is really important. And we are moving forward! The Bukavu Women's Trauma Healing and Care Center Committee has created rooms to work in, and we raised enough money to buy ten sewing machines. I started co-leading workshops in three Congolese towns on healing trauma and empowering these women. More importantly, we're creating an organization that can finance their income-producing projects, and we're fund-raising to build a school for their children.

"It's one thing to read about this in newspapers or online. But to slowly become friends with the women who are valiantly rebuilding their lives after having gone through violence and rape—that changed me. This project became much more than a good deed. I started taking it very personally, and I made it my personal mission to support these amazing women.

"Teaching assertiveness there is tricky, to say the least, and the victims need to be convinced that their misfortune is not their fault. You could say we are starting at ground zero, since so many of them are ashamed and take responsibility for being raped and abused.

"You have to understand that this project isn't over—it is ongoing, and I am continuing to learn more about my role as a leader every day. Nothing is static; everything is changing all the time, so how I thought of myself as a leader last week is different from how I think about it today. The forms of service and the mission keep changing with each new project, but my personal commitment stays the same.

"Maybe in its ultimate form it's my belief that by working together to stop violence, we can expand consciousness to a critical mass, shifting from a culture of world violence to one of peace. My Life Purpose has become to work toward an end to violence against women and children worldwide. My Stake in the Congo is, 'Empowered women working collectively as an international community have the power to heal the deepest trauma and build safe communities for themselves and their children.' We have the power to change the world. And I am watching that happen."

Emily knew Victoria was no superwoman, and yet she kept on heading back again to change the world, one small African town at a time. But Emily didn't feel any such great calling. The numbness was back.

In the staff room that evening, Zeke pushed back in the brown leather Barcalounger, took a sip of his Red Zinger tea, yawned, and asked, "So, how do you think it's going?"

Stella walked over to the window and looked out over the calm Pacific Ocean and into a sky alight with tiny stars. At first she was silent, and she let that silence hang there. Then she turned and faced Zeke.

"The room is getting it. I love this group—they seem so eager to learn it's electric out there. But our dance sucks. Look, I know we didn't do all that well the last time we worked together, but we stumbled through. Today it was worse. Every time I opened my mouth, it felt like you started talking over me. You kept stepping in to run the Zeke Show."

Zeke straightened up his chair. He wasn't angry, but he saw things very differently. "Look, I respect you, Stella. But I take one hundred percent responsibility for the room. And I know you take one hundred percent responsibility for the room as well. But I won't play small to make room for you. I am not going to wait around for you. If you want to lead the room, then do it."

Stella sighed. "I have no problem stepping in and leading. And look, I sure don't want you doing stupid 'handoffs' to show how generous you are. But, damn it, trust that the participants will get what we are trying to present to them. Stop jumping in so fast when I am practically in the middle of a sentence. Get it?"

Unexpectedly, Zeke smiled. "Okay. I get it. I like strong women! Kick me if you see me jumping all over you. But don't expect me to wait around until you figure out what you want to say. Deal?"

Stella shook her head. "Ouch. That seemed a little patronizing. I don't think we are aligned yet. Look, we both want our dance to inspire the participants, right?"

"Yes, I want us to love working together, and we sure aren't there yet."

"Me too. Right now, I need to know you have heard me and aren't just trying to end this conversation."

"Look, I don't like being called patronizing. Okay, maybe I was trying to rush this a little. So, you're feeling that I don't trust you because I jump in too often. Is that it?"

Stella said, "Closer. But I still feel like it's the Zeke Show, instead of the Stella and Zeke Show."

"Okay, I hear that. Are you hearing what I said?"

Stella said, "I get that you are not going to roll out a red carpet and play on your trumpet while I am deciding what to say. So I will jump in more, and you can let me take the room. Okay?"

"I don't want a one-man band up there either. So I'll pay attention to that. Let's talk tomorrow night, and you tell me if it feels like there's more room for you out there."

Stella nodded. "Deal!"

The next morning, Emily was definitely not feeling numb anymore. In fact, she longed for some numbness. Right now, she would be happy just dozing off in front of her fireplace with a new book of sudoku puzzles on her lap and a big glass of pinot noir beside her. Instead, her armpits were wet and she wanted to cry because she was hanging on a "ladder" made of rope and rounded log "steps." She was stuck about five feet off the ground.

Today's high ropes course was forcing her to confront one of her greatest fears, her fear of heights. In this first event, the challenge was to climb the free-swinging log ladder to a platform high in the air. Even though she wore a full climbing harness and was always on belay, it didn't change anything. Once she had climbed up the first five log steps, she froze. Clinging to the rough bark at the fifth step, she felt like an utter fool. Finally she gave up and inched her way back down to the ground.

To add to her embarrassment, she started crying when she got off that first step. Stella signaled Zeke to manage the group while she put her arm around Emily and walked away from the ropes area, over to a fallen log overlooking a brook. "I fail at almost everything I try these days," Emily said through her tears.

"Me too," Stella replied gently.

"Oh, right! I don't think so."

"Let me tell you a story about me and failure. I was raised on Chicago's South Side. Mancusi is my father's name. The name my grandmother gave me means something like 'Annoyingly Curious Raven.' I spent every summer on the reservation."

Seeing Emily's look of confusion, Stella continued, "That's the Bad River Reservation, up in northern Wisconsin. My mother was full-blooded Chippewa. But for a while I disowned that world. First, I went to school in Chicago and tried on about five majors and as many careers. Then I decided that I was going to be a millionaire. I took after my competitive Italian American dad. I drove myself to take on the financial industry.

"I was moving up the ranks in the bank where I worked, not letting anything or anyone stop me. I wanted to be the first Native woman president of that company. I finally hammered up against the glass ceiling that almost every woman in that industry hits.

"I failed, again and again. My aggression, which was seen at first as a healthy competitive spirit, was now being labeled as resentful bitchiness. For the first time in my life, my job ratings began to go down. So I started drinking and partying pretty hard to cover up the knowledge that I was a failure.

"One hung over morning, I looked in the mirror and saw this white streak in my hair. I mean, it had been there a long time, and I kind of liked it. But that morning I remembered where it came from. It was the same streak that my grandmother had. I called her Kiki. Don't know why. Anyway, touching that lock of white with my hand and looking at my empty, bloodshot eyes, I remembered what Kiki told me the last time we saw each other.

"'Raven,' she said, 'you are going to throw yourself into their world. And you will be successful at that. I know you will. You are going to get it all: nice cars, nice clothes, big televisions. But you won't find peace. Peace is not for sale. Sooner or later you are going to start to hear another song, not just the song of money. That other song is going to stop you in your tracks. Come back and see me when you hear that other music.'

"So it finally happened. She was right. I got in my car and drove to the res. She was so glad to see me. The first thing she said was, 'Raven, I'm so glad you are here. You didn't lose your soul.' And in that moment I realized that I almost had. My grand success had been at a horrible cost. Sure, I had clawed my way up the ladder, but I had failed at living my purpose and had sacrificed everything that defined me. I hadn't heard a loon in years. I hadn't watched the moon rise or plunged into ice-cold lake water. I hadn't stood beside my mother as she cooked, singing as I chopped the vegetables for her. I had become cut off from my land and my people. I had failed at the job of living my life. So I phoned in my resignation to the bank and spent the next two years back on my land, learning from my grandmother.

"These days, I know that each failure teaches me something I need to know. I always remember what Winston Churchill said: 'Success is the ability to go from failure to failure without losing your enthusiasm.' Emily, there is no leadership without risk, and there is no risk without failure.

"I risked when I headed up that job ladder at the bank and left my childhood behind. Then I risked again when I threw it all away and headed down the path that brought me here. You are here to learn how to lean into your own mistakes and failures without having them knock you off balance or pull you away from your Stake. Right now you're learning to stop taking failure personally. And you're starting to see how to keep your failures from confirming some stupid Level One conversation that says, *Emily is a failure. Na-na-na-na-na-na!*"

While Stella was talking, Emily stopped crying and just listened intently. She even smiled at that last crack.

Stella went on, "It's like being up there on that ladder. I was scared up there, too, when I did it. But when I am moving forward, clearly oriented to my Stake, I realize that every step I take could be a mistake or a failure. Whether it is successful or not, that step will inform me of the next one I need to take. I like to call it failing forward. It's the only way a baby learns to walk or a leader learns to lead."

Emily had another chance to practice on the next event: the Bridge. She had seen several people topple over and fall. This time it was Allen, the minister, who froze, just as Emily had in the last event. As they tackled the event, each of them was strapped in their harness and on belay, so there was no real danger, yet fear immobilized some of the participants and sabotaged others.

As Emily waited for her turn, she thought, *This is my life. Right here. How many times have I just refused to even climb the tree? How many days have I looked out over what faced me and decided to stay safe on my comfortable platform? I wanted to be in theater in high school, but I decided there was no money in it. So I turned my back on it. I knew my marriage was over years before it*

ended, and four years ago I met Aaron, a wonderful man who
wanted to know me better. I sent him away because it was easier
to say, "Sorry, I'm already married." So I chose to stay with what
was familiar, even though what was familiar was an empty
marriage. And look where that got me. This is my life. It's crap. I
want more!

Emily was still terrified, but this time she was not immobilized.
She made it up the tree in what felt like record time. As she stood on
the platform, she said to herself, *Not me! They are* not *hauling me*
down off this platform. She let go of the safety of the tree trunk.
With a big breath, she began moving along the rope, trying not to
look at the ground far below. Just one step at a time. Everything
slowed down.

She was quite startled when the ropes instructor grabbed her
hand. She had made it to the other side! A huge round of whistles
and applause came up from below. She looked down at the group of
smiling faces looking up at her, and she laughed, threw both fists up
in the air, and shouted, "Yes!" Cheers of admiration and approval
echoed through the forest.

Just after lunch on the second day, Stella and Zeke gave the
group some surprising news.

"Okay, you guys," said Zeke, "it's time to make you an official
tribe." Around the room, eyebrows raised, mouths opened, and
unspoken curiosity filled the air.

"You heard us," said Stella. "Every Leadership group gets a
unique name and character. We want you all to be able to be totally
connected with your fellow tribe mates here, so we give you a tribe
name and invite you to embody the spirit of that name. So, from
this moment on, you are all . . ." She paused for effect.

"Unicorns!" said Zeke, with a grin and a nod to Stella.

Now the questions came thick and fast. "Why Unicorns?" "What's a Unicorn?" "When did you decide . . .?"

Zeke held up his hand for silence. When everyone was quiet, he explained, "Unicorns are magical beasts with many special qualities. For example, unicorns are considered to be wild woodland animals. They're usually associated with characteristics of purity and grace, so they bring peace and honor into the world. In the Middle Ages, people believed that they could make bad water drinkable and could heal sickness.

"So we expect that each of you will find your own way to embody the spirit of the unicorn into your own leadership journey, both here in the program and for the rest of your lives, after you take your own leadership into the world. Every tribe finds its own way of living up to its special character, and we know you all will, too."

The next day, Zeke introduced one of the most ridiculous assessment experiences Emily had ever been through.

"Part of our approach to leadership comes from the field of acting. And when you think about it, an actor and a leader have the same task: to create an intended impact on a group of people. Today we are going to utilize a tool created for actors to help you learn to lead from your greatest strength as a person.

"Back in the mid-1980s, Henry Kimsey-House, a co-creator of this program, was working at a career consulting firm for actors, singers, and dancers in New York City. He focused on helping performers prepare for auditions—"

Stella broke in, "Zeke doesn't know this, but I did some theater back when I was in college. I remember how awful auditions were, how I tried so hard to give the directors what I thought they wanted to see. If a role was for a young mother, I would dress up in my best young-mom outfit and try like hell to put on what I thought was a young-mom smile and exude a young-mom attitude. Like I had the faintest idea what that was! I was twenty and very single. I wish Henry had been around for me back then!"

"Yes," said Zeke, "and what Stella didn't realize, but what Henry Kimsey-House had figured out, was what the man or woman who sat on the other side of the desk was really looking for. All directors are looking for is someone who's 'real,' someone with 'stage presence,' someone who's confident and certain in who they are. Most of the time, those determinations can be made in minutes, sometimes as the actor walks through the door, before anyone says, 'Boo.'

"Henry wanted the performers he was coaching to get a sense of how they were seen when they were in their strength and power. He wanted them to know what was engaging and entertaining about them when they were just being themselves.

"So he created a system, a sort of language of personality, to define the different ways in which people—actors, in that case—make an impression with their personality. He wasn't interested in how people defined themselves; rather, he focused on how they could intentionally and powerfully impact others. He defined seven different ways in which a person can make an authentic impact, and he called them 'types.'

"The first type was the Danger type. The energetic impact of a Danger type on others is one of stillness, edginess, and discomfort. Think of the quality of the air just before a thunderstorm. There is electricity in the air, a sense of pending action, yet the air is very still. This is the impact of the Danger type.

"One often shifts in one's seat, feeling a little uncomfortable, in the presence of a Danger type. Telling the hard truth in a calm, matter-of-fact way, the Danger type helps us face what we sometimes fear. And while the Danger types' unswerving, icy-cool energy can sometimes be uncomfortable to be with, it also assures us that nothing will be avoided, so we get a sense of trust."

Stella turned in her chair and gave Zeke a gentle kick in the shins. As he chuckled, she turned back and said, "Next comes the Sex type. The energetic impact of a Sex type on others is one of physicality and movement. The Sex type makes others more aware of their own bodies and their physical sensations. When a Sex type is around, the temperature is hot. Their energy is often aggressive. It reaches out to you, and you may feel an urge to move your body, or, at a minimum, you will be much more aware of what you are experiencing within your own body. Sex types themselves are often moving their bodies, their arms, their hands.

"Another of Henry's types is the Beauty type. The Beauty type's energetic impact on others is reverence, depth, coolness, and stillness. Think of the placid surface of a pristine mountain lake; it's cool, clear, and inviting. But don't be diverted by the words Henry used to name the types. The Beauty type is not about being physically beautiful—it's about bringing a sense of deep appreciation for all things. In the presence of a Beauty type, we feel drawn in. We become aware of our emotions, often feeling moved by what the Beauty type is saying or doing. We feel a sense of grace, dignity, and divinity in the presence of a person who is on type as a Beauty."

"Here's one of my favorites," said Zeke: "the Charm type. The energetic impact of a Charm type is warmth and connection. When someone is fully expressed as a Charm type, we feel more at ease; we're relaxed and often prepared to have fun. Charm types are frequently able to be irreverent or tell the 'hard truth' in a casual, easy way, so that others can hear it without being offended. In the presence of a Charm type, we want to hang out, be connected, have a cup of coffee, and enjoy the world around us.

"Follow the laughter, and you will probably find a Humor type. The energetic impact of a Humor type is lightness, but Humor types are not necessarily funny. However, they do a lot to shift the energy in a group from heaviness or consternation to ease and lightness.

Humor types differ from Charm types because their impact on others is coolness and amusement, rather than the warmth and engagement of a Charm type. In a work situation, when a team gets stuck in a quagmire over a difficult issue and things are starting to feel grim, just like turning on a light in a dark room, the Humor type will say or do something that effortlessly shifts the energy to an easier, more fun-loving experience for everyone."

"One of the most interesting of Henry's types is the Eccentric type," Stella continued.

Zeke laughed. "*You* don't always think it's so interesting."

Stella laughed with him. "Zeke here is a prime example of the Eccentric type. The energetic impact of an Eccentric type is angularity, unpredictability, and delight. Other descriptors of this type include quirkiness or twitchiness. Eccentric types often see the world in a very different, more unconventional way than the rest of us. Sometimes they move their bodies with a delightful awkwardness that's very compelling, despite its oddity. In the presence of an Eccentric type, we non-Eccentrics often feel a bit on guard because we don't know what unexpected and strange thing will happen next. It is very interesting, and sometimes a bit disturbing, leading with one—believe me! Eccentric types help the rest of us appreciate the weirdness of things."

Zeke went on, "And finally, a place where all these types meet is the Intelligence type. The Intelligence type's energetic impact is smoothness, clarity, and competence. The strength of this type isn't about being intellectually smart; it is about conveying a sense of capability and often includes curiosity. When you are in the presence of an Intelligence type, the air feels clear. Even when an Intelligence type has no idea of the answer to a thorny question, those around him or her will feel they are in capable hands and the issue will be competently resolved. The energetic temperature around an Intelligence type is cool. There isn't much drama or emotional turmoil; instead, there's a sense of ease and stability."

Stella broke in, "Knowing this system, showing up in my strength would have made such a difference in that audition I told you about. If you haven't guessed yet, I am a Sex type, and if I had shown up to that young-mother audition in the fullness of who I am—appealing, a touch bawdy, and intimate—I would have nailed it. I would have been irresistible!"

Zeke picked up, "So the people who created this program decided to incorporate Henry's typing work from the acting workshops because they wanted leaders who were certain and confident in their true selves. They wanted to train leaders to know exactly who they were and how they were perceived when they were in their strength. And they wanted to help leaders learn how to remove barriers to their authentic, full self-expression."

Stella smiled, nodded at Zeke, and then said, "So now you're all going to get the flavor of this system firsthand."

When it was her turn for the typing process, Emily stood in front of the group. The leaders asked her to do several odd improvisational exercises, like "Act out the flavor of your favorite dessert" and "Be a shopping cart." After she had tried these and several others, everyone in the group voted on what they thought her type was from the list: Beauty, Danger, Sex, Charm, Eccentric, Intelligence, or Humor.

These types had no connection to any assessment system Emily had ever heard of. She expected to be classified as an Intelligence type and was very confused when the room voted overwhelmingly to type her as a Beauty. She knew she was no beauty. She was overweight, out of shape, and ordinary looking. She shared her confusion with the leaders.

Zeke explained, "No, Emily, Beauty has nothing to do with good looks. It has everything to do with your impact on the people in the room. When a Beauty type steps up to lead, he or she cools the room in a way that makes everyone breathe a little easier. With Beauty types setting the tone, there is more room for everyone to look deeper into themselves, to feel more. There is kind of an easy blue chill that soothes conflict. Everyone feels deeply received and accepted by the leader who is a Beauty type."

Although Emily still felt that she had been wrongly typed, she bit back her opinion and sat down. But inside, she was taking a jaundiced view of this whole exercise. She'd had enough clinical experience to know that when you diagnose or assess people, once they find out how you label them, they will seek to live that out, consciously or unconsciously, and to fit themselves into whatever they think that label means. She had already decided that this was just one more way of creating an artificial box to fit people into.

She couldn't help secretly agreeing with Olivia when she went ballistic over her own typing. "There is no way I am a Sex type! You people are crazy!" Olivia was incensed, standing with her hands on her hips, glaring out at everyone in the room just as soon as they had voted. "That is just stupid, and a little insulting. Zeke, Stella, fix this! The group is wrong."

Stella said, "Olivia, this is a leadership moment for you. Take a breath and step out of your opinion of yourself. There is some information in your environment that might be useful for you to take in. Your tribe mates voted overwhelmingly for this type. So, first of all, put out of your mind everything you're thinking about what the words *Sex type* mean. Believe me, I know how you feel. I felt the same way when I was told that I was a Sex type.

"It has nothing to do with promiscuity or immoral behavior. It's about the quality of energy you bring to your life, with no judgment attached. Look at you up there, hands on hips. You use your body powerfully to communicate what you feel. That is what the rest of the room is seeing."

Zeke reminded her, "Don't forget that this phase of the typing process is only the beginning phase. People often react immediately to the label or, even worse, try to fit into the label. Bad idea. Right now, it's difficult for you and for everyone in this room to know what everyone else is looking at. In a way, this is actually the opposite of a rigid, well-defined, absolute label. It's an invitation to experiment with a part of you that may be able to have a powerful effect on the people you lead.

"We're inviting you to discover a part of yourself you might not know very well. It's not a diagnosis or a straitjacket. You'll understand so much more about what this really means by the end of the second retreat. So right now, just let yourself be confused and a little pissed, but stay open to what you might learn about yourself. There is something here that the room saw clearly in you. We want you to find out what it is."

Brainwashing, Emily thought.

When everyone had been through the process, they gathered in groups according to type. Emily was 90 percent sure the system was bogus, but as she talked with the other three Beauty types, she noticed that her judgments began to soften. In her Beauty group the conversation flowed naturally—no disconnects and no competition for dominance. Every one of them just seemed to know exactly when to share, and they were all completely attuned to each other.

There were even some weird similarities. Everyone in the Beauty group had had an experience of interacting with a group or an audience and saying something that left everyone speechless. That often left them feeling as if they had somehow screwed up. As they talked about it, they came to realize that, in reality, they had probably just given everyone something really juicy to think about, but often the learning came from a rich silence that seemed to emanate from them. It was as though they created a still, sacred space around them without even trying to.

There were other unexpected similarities. They all seemed to have access to an almost chilly, cool temperature, a layer of energy that they could use like a shield to keep others from really seeing them. It might be charming, serene, highly competent, or very well put together. It was always polished in a certain way. They all hated being perceived as a mess.

Emily discovered that she actually felt more comfortable talking with these three people than she had at any earlier point in the retreat. Somehow they felt as if they were all from the same family. Perhaps the deepest link they all shared was their sense of living at a distance from life, as though they were in it but not fully immersed. They often sensed a thin barrier between them and others. One Beauty, an Asian American woman named Anna, told about an evening when that barrier finally came down and she and her lover had an amazingly intimate night together. That was the only time Emily could not relate to what another Beauty type was saying. She had never let anyone in that close.

Even though she was starting to find it interesting, she still had serious reservations about the validity of this assessment system. It wasn't until she left the group for a few minutes that the validity went way up. On her way to the restroom, she walked past the group of Eccentric types. She listened in on them for a few moments and realized how glad she was that she hadn't ended up with them. But she already knew that. When the Eccentric group had all stood in front of the room, she had started to feel edgy and anxious. They seemed to have no manners and very little concern for the impression they were making. And they all acted odd—sometimes very funny, but still odd. They had made the whole room a little nervous. Except, of course, the other oblivious Eccentrics.

Emily listened to them talking about their self-image issues. Allen Bowers, the minister, was saying, "Don't tell anyone, but I couldn't care less about what other people think of me! Most pastors I know get their knickers all wadded up trying to please their governing board, their congregation, their superiors. I figure I'll just serve God and let him handle the details. Or her, if God is really female. Or it, for all you Buddhists. Or them, which is probably more like it. The committee formerly known as God."

His comments were met with laughter and a shower of agreements. "I know! Who cares what other people think of us? If I go to a party and everyone looks boring, I'll go sit in a corner and read a good book. Screw them." Everyone laughed.

Then Frank, a skinny and extremely tall corporate attorney, said, "I know we are laughing. But sometimes the reaction we get from others does feel a little weird, doesn't it? We don't feel odd, yet other people either laugh at us or tend to shy away from us like we have a disease or something."

This was a very different conversation from the one they were having in the Beauty group. Hmm, definitely not Emily's cup of tea. But they seemed to be very happy together. Perhaps there *was* some value in this seemingly unprofessional typing system.

That **evening**, Emily began to see how this odd classification system might actually serve her. It was Story Night. The tribe was sitting in a circle, and the two leaders had left them alone to self-manage. Their assignment was to spend the next two evenings telling stories to each other. Everyone was expected to participate.

Emily so wanted just to go hide in her room. She wasn't up to intimate sharing. And then, as soon as they all sat down together, chaos erupted. Phil Serrito, the high-powered corporate-executive type, wanted to parcel out the time exactly and have people sign up for a segment. Isabel Lopez, another corporate type, met Phil face-to-face, arguing in her shrill voice that they should just let the process unfold without any imposed structure. Allen Bowers, the minister, was nervously trying to make peace between those two by calling for a vote. Emily felt this whole mess was very wrong. This should be a night of safe, open sharing, not one filled with tyrants and co-dependents fighting for control.

Then she stopped judging everyone who spoke and just listened to what Allen was saying. She could hear his sincerity, as well as his desire for everyone to play nice. Finally, she'd had enough. This bickering had to stop now.

She interrupted the three-way debate. "Stop, please. No, I mean it! Can everyone just be silent for a minute and breathe? Breathe!" She looked around. Things got very quiet, and quite a few people looked relieved that someone had interrupted the conflict. But she noticed that Phil looked annoyed and seemed antsy. He looked ready to return to the attack. "Good," she said. "Now, let's just look around at each other for a minute without speaking, and without thinking about our opinions and about how you are right and someone else is wrong. Just look around." She watched Phil's face slowly soften as he looked at the others. "Good. Whew. Doesn't that feel better? Now, let's all just gently let go of being attached to having the right answer. Who would like to speak to what approach might best serve all of us?"

And with that intervention, the energy shifted and cooled down. The conflict-charged atmosphere started to dissolve. Phil smiled and said, "Okay, let's try Isabel's idea and see how it goes. We can always try something else if that doesn't work."

Allen laughed. "Well, Emily, now I see how a Beauty type leads a room. Thank you. Okay, how about I go first and we'll just see how the evening unfolds from there?"

"You know, I tell stories all the time," he began. "You might even say that, as a minister, I make my living telling and retelling the most important story I know. But I don't want to do that here. I want you to know me, so I have to tell a story I really don't want to tell. But I know that if I don't tell it, I will spend the whole time we are together trying to cover it up. I haven't talked about this before in a group outside the program, and I'm a little scared, but here goes." Allen paused for a moment, took a deep breath, and composed himself. After a few moments, he began.

"Hi, I'm Allen, and I am an alcoholic. For those of you who haven't been in a meeting or haven't watched some reality-TV show about it, those are the words you use to introduce yourself at Alcoholics Anonymous. I should know. I have been saying them for seven years. I drank from the time I was a teenager, hiding a bottle of scotch under my bed. I drank through seminary, sobering up only during exams.

"I'm an Episcopalian priest, and I was a master at looking cold sober. I could give an entire sermon, stay afterward to talk church business, even counsel my parishioners, and then I would wake up Monday morning with no memories of Sunday and only hazy recollections of the drinking I had done on Saturday night.

"No one knew. I was married and had a wonderful ten-year-old daughter, Kimberly. Now I'm separated, probably soon to be divorced. An affair with a woman in my congregation nearly ruined my career. It was all kept secret from everyone except my wife. She left me. If sin means estrangement from God, I was the worst sinner in my flock. If my wife hadn't been so ashamed and had opened her mouth about it, my career could have easily been ruined.

"I felt like a complete hypocrite, but I still could not stop myself from drinking. Reports were reaching my bishop about my work, and it felt like the whole house of cards that I called my life was collapsing.

"In the midst of this emotional turmoil, my parish secretary came up to me one day and said, 'Allen, I started going to AA meetings last month, and I haven't had a drink in thirty days. I hope you don't think I'm being a complete meddler, but I'm going to a noon meeting, and you could come with me if you wanted to check it out. It's an open meeting, which means they welcome anyone who is interested in AA, whether or not they might think they have a drinking problem. You wouldn't have to say a word. At the very least, it could help you understand some of your parishioners who struggle with alcoholism. Would you like to come with me?'

"I was too tired to be defensive. I went with her, realizing that I was actually almost at the end of my rope. A man who was just a stranger to me at that time spent the first fifteen minutes of the meeting telling his story of drinking and recovery. It scared the hell out of me! It was eerie: the same bottle of scotch under his bed, the same survival games at the university, and the same downward career spiral. If *he* called himself an alcoholic, that could mean only one thing for me. I have been going back to those meetings ever since, and that man who spoke at that first meeting is now my sponsor.

"I can't say it has been easy. I have had two bad slips since that day. My bishop pulled me out of my parish and put me in an all-administrative capacity. He's probably figured out at least some of my mess. I see my daughter every other weekend. When I go home after this retreat, there will likely be a big, fat envelope from my wife's lawyer waiting for me. But no matter what happens, I'll keep going back to the meetings. I have a therapist, and I am clean and sober today. I just wanted you to know that about me."

As Emily listened to Allen, something inside her began to melt. She stopped holding herself apart from the group. She stopped pretending that she was just there to learn some new skills. She felt herself actually caring. It was a warm feeling, but also she was a little scared about letting these people into her heart.

Olivia went next. "Thanks, Allen. I love how open you were."

Three people in the tribe said, "Speak louder, Olivia."

Olivia said, in a slightly louder voice, "Oh, sorry. I guess I have to use my classroom voice. So, I want to tell you all about something I did, because I think it led directly to my signing up for this program. I don't really see myself as a leader type very much. I mean, I'm a schoolteacher, so I guess that is a form of leadership. But it's a pretty constrained one, believe me!

"Anyway, two years ago I decided to run a marathon. It was weird, because I am not an athlete or a runner, or anything like that. I think I did it because when I told my sister that running a marathon was on my bucket list, she laughed at me.

"That did it! I trained for six months, crawling out of my nice, cozy bed, feeding my kitty, strapping on my running shoes, and hitting the track by six every morning. I must have been nuts. But I sure got in shape!

"I ran my marathon in Oregon, on a nice, flat course around a bay in Newport. It was a lot more grueling than I imagined, but I was still okay when I got to a spot about two miles from the finish line. There was this old guy who'd stopped. He was just leaning against a tree, looking upset or something. So I stopped running and walked over to him to see if he was okay.

"'I'm fine,' he said. 'You go on. I am just at the end of my rope, that's all. It's time to hang it up.'

"You know, my normal self would have just gone back into the race. But something kept me there—I think it was the lonely, defeated look in his eyes. So I said to him, 'Hi. My name is Olivia. You know, this is my first marathon, so I am not trying to set some record or anything. Can I just hang out with you for a while? I need the rest.'

"His name was Mike. We talked for a while, and then I kind of coaxed him into accompanying me just a little farther. And we started walking along, and talking, and before we noticed, the banner marking the end of the course was right in front of us. You should have seen him! The beaten old man literally ran across the finish line with his arms in the air, with the biggest grin you ever saw. We hugged and cried for at least five minutes—I kid you not!

"After he thanked me, we said good-bye and I never saw him again. But something really precious happened for me that day: I saw how I could transform someone who had given up into someone absolutely beaming because he was a winner. And believe me, if you have never run a marathon, I'm telling you, just making it over that finish line for the first time is a huge victory! I want more moments like that, of changing people's lives."

Then Isabel stood up. "Thank you both. Ah, yes, Allen—secrets at work. Can I join you there? You kind of cleared the way for me to talk about something I need you all to know. I am a gay woman, and nowadays I'm proud of it. But that hasn't always been the case. I came from a very traditional Latino family. For most of my adolescence, I tried so hard to look like I cared about dating men, but my heart was actually somewhere else. I was ashamed of my true feelings, until my first woman lover opened my eyes. What a relief that was! I couldn't wait to tell my family the truth. Big mistake.

"I was twenty-two when I told my parents. My father stopped speaking to me. My mother would wait until he left the house to call me. Five years later, my father died of a heart attack, and I've never been able to heal that split.

"I still basically live a lie. I am the executive director of a very traditional, Christian-based nonprofit agency. In this age of bankrupt public agencies, we're doing amazing work getting disabled people off the streets and often even back to work. I love my job. But if they knew I was a lesbian, they would hand me a cardboard box to pack up my desk, and I would be out the door.

"It's such a relief to be in a group of people who I know will respect my confidentiality, and where I can be out and open. Thank you, Unicorns!"

Something was happening in that room. Emily had sat in on plenty of encounter groups before, where people bared their secrets to strangers. But this was different. These people were not sharing to a group of strangers they would never see again, in order to get some catharsis. They were sharing to people they would be living with for most of a year, perhaps for years to come. Maybe they were sharing because they thought that holding themselves back, hiding away some part of who they were in order to be nice or to be liked, would eat away at their power to lead authentically. At least, Emily knew that was true for her. This wasn't some assignment handed to them. It was a process they were creating all by themselves, an exercise in honesty and openness for the sake of being able to play full out for the rest of their time in this program. Emily knew that if Allen and Isabel had been so brave, she was going to have to speak from her heart. She wanted this group to know her, too.

"Hello, everyone," she said. "I need to tell you about lilacs."

That night, Emily lay in bed, unable to sleep. She could hear her roommate's gentle breathing, but she was too churned up to sleep, and her head was buzzing. Eventually, she got up quietly, wrapped her thick robe around her, and walked down to the main hall. At this late hour there was no one else there, but the fire was still flickering. She made a cup of hot chocolate and sat by the embers, thinking.

This stuff was actually starting to make sense! That circular diagram actually mapped out something real. She saw in a new light the Leadership Model that the leaders had presented on the first day. In that night's story-group meeting, she had followed it unconsciously, like a map.

Her Stake had been for everyone to have the freedom to share openly and in their own way. When she had tuned in to the Level Three atmosphere at the start of the storytelling session, she had experienced it as contentious and competitive, definitely not a safe environment for sharing.

So she had had an urge, one that she acted on, to stop all the arguing and to help the group get grounded and aligned with what was really important. She had stayed alert and had seen that after the group got quiet, Phil was still not on board. So she had acted on another urge and had everyone look around. Then she had seen him appear to step off his position. Finally, without her even needing to tell them her Stake, Emily had noticed that the group was much more attuned to it, and she had turned the responsibility for what came next back to the group.

She was beginning to see that a leader doesn't lead by imposing her will or structure on the group, as both Phil and Isabel had been trying to do. And a leader doesn't lead by trying to find compromises, as Allen had tried to do. She still wasn't clear what, exactly, she herself had done, but she knew it was something very different from either of those two strategies.

The next day, when they were debriefing about the previous night's storytelling exercise, Emily began to talk about her experience with the group. Zeke smiled as she told how she had started by doubting herself and judging the tribe, then had begun listening closely to Allen and had eventually succeeded in redirecting the tribe's energy.

He said, "Remember the spaceship exercise? How all we saw was Emily's Destructive Self up there, whining for help? Now she is showing us how a leader uses Level Two and Level Three Awareness."

Stella said, "Yes, let's hang out here a little while. Let's talk some more about what those terms mean. Level One Awareness is all about what is going on inside you. Right now, you might be wishing these chairs were more comfortable, or wishing you had a second cup of coffee, or grumpy that your roommate snores. Those are all examples of Level One Awareness.

"Level Two Awareness occurs when you open up and let the other person into your own field of awareness. You are no longer just focusing on yourself. You are curious about and open to the other person.

"What I'm hearing is that when Emily joined the group last night, she was feeling very self-conscious—a Level One place. But then she focused her attention and awareness on Allen. She moved away from judging him, started listening to what he was saying, and sensed underneath his words to what he was feeling.

"Once I can get all of that negative chatter out of my way, I don't need to project or assume that I know who that person is opposite me. I can focus my attention over there and truly see, hear, and begin to understand that other person. Level Two is that feeling of a conduit or channel that opens up between us. Sometimes everything else in the world melts away in the intensity of that focus and attention. With that kind of focus comes a powerful empathy, a sense of clearly seeing and knowing this person opposite me, a sense of timelessness that happens when two people truly connect."

Emily nodded. "Yes, I noticed something happening with Allen, but it really came home to me with Phil. Once everyone stopped arguing, it was like I could look inside Phil and see exactly when his energy started to shift and when he started to soften his position."

Zeke picked up on that comment. "Yes, you were finely tuned to Phil using your Level Two Awareness. And it also sounds like you were using Level Three Awareness. This one is a bit harder to explain.

"Some of the martial arts teach you to focus on two things at the same time. You focus on the fist coming at you, and at the same time you open your focus to let in everything that's happening around you and your opponent. That is how, in those kung fu films, the master can handle a group of attackers coming at him all at the same time. He seems to effortlessly move in a way that disarms or immobilizes all of his opponents.

"Martial artists call that being able to hold a soft focus and a hard focus at the same time. Level Three Awareness is like that soft focus—being able to create an awareness of everything around you and the spaces in between, and being able to direct your focus in an instant to where an attack is coming from, and responding to the attack without losing that soft, three-sixty-degree focus."

Stella said, "It sounds like Emily was doing that last night. She was aware in a hard-focused way of Phil and his desire to move things forward. She was also aware of Allen and Isabel. Her antennas were so open that she was also aware of the whole room, and of the relief that the silent participants felt when she exercised leadership and stopped the bickering. From that place, she was able to transform the atmosphere of conflict in a way that made Allen, and everyone else in the room, feel more connected and less competitive."

Zeke added. "Level Three Awareness is the ability to sense the space, the whole room, and all of the energies that are moving around in it. That awareness is not just the sum of your noticing each person in the room. It's all that and so much more—it's the ability to read the emotional energies in a room and to sense what's going on in the space between everyone, rather than what's going on with just one or two people individually.

"That may sound a bit mystical at first. You see, most of us stop at Level Two Awareness. Some leaders have developed an ability to do what I call 'machine gun Level Two,' a kind of rapid-fire reading and summing up of what the individuals are feeling or the level of their attention. These unfortunate leaders may think they are reading the energy in the room, but often they are surprised when things explode or go in unpredictable ways.

"When you're able to open up your Level Three Awareness, you aren't surprised by the energies swirling around you. In fact, you're able to dance with them. When you aren't knocking yourself senseless running around, trying to take care of every single detail or manage everyone's reactions, even chaos turns out to be an opportunity."

Stella leaned forward in her chair. "One of the most important distinguishing features of our Leadership Model is that it focuses on the space that the leader moves in, the space the leader creates in, and the space the leader leads in. We call that space the Level Three. The Level Three includes everything that's going on in the space, and the space itself. But for goodness' sake, don't worry if all this sounds like gobbledygook. This whole Level Three thing will get much clearer in our third retreat."

Emily smiled. "I kind of get what you mean. I could focus clearly on Phil and Allen and Isabel while at the same time sensing the temperature of everyone else in the room. This is going to sound a little silly, but it was almost as if the group was using me to guide it to a way of working together that was perfect. It wasn't so much like grabbing the group and pushing it the way I wanted to, but more like speaking the truth that the group wanted to hear."

"Exactly!" said Stella. "You were speaking to what the Level Three needed in that moment. Now, with this new language, we can revisit the model and begin to see more clearly how it works. Let's take another trip around it." She walked over to the circular diagram of the Co-Active Leadership Model.

The Co-Active® Leadership Model

"As we said already, you can pretty much jump onto the model anywhere you want, once the Leader's Stake is planted. So let's jump on at *URGE*. We often begin things based on an urge, an instinct, or a reaction. The leader may feel a strong Level One urge, from that grounded Level One place, for something that she wants to do, some action that she wants to take. Although she probably didn't consciously acknowledge it, Emily's Stake was probably something like, 'This group will grow if everyone gets to share in their own way tonight.' Her self-awareness probably included a lot of discomfort with the battle that had started, together with a desire to have something more creative happen, something that would engage her in the exercise."

Emily nodded. This chart, which had looked so abstract two days ago, was beginning to make sense. She settled back into her chair and let herself focus on Stella's assessment.

"Now, if the group had just started by sharing and being open, there would have been no need for Emily to lead anything. The work of the group would have progressed, and the group would already be aligned around her Stake. But that was not what happened. Instead, a battle for leadership broke out, and the work of the group stopped dead in its tracks. When work stops, or when the wrong work is getting done, a leader is needed. And you are that leader when you act on your urge."

Zeke continued, "Maybe Emily also had an urge to walk out of the room and go to bed. But I am guessing that just before she spoke, her urge was, 'This isn't getting anywhere, and I need to do something about it.' Her Destructive Self might have won the day by saying, 'Phil and Isabel are fighting again, those stubborn, pigheaded jerks. I have to fix this!' Or, worse, 'There is a fight going on, but it's not my fight, so I will just sit here quietly and disappear, even though I have an urge to do something.' If she had acted from either of those urges, the mess would probably have gotten even messier.

"But she acted from a deep sense that now was the time for action. She acted from this urge to take responsibility for getting the group back on task. The leader marries that Level One urge with the awareness that she's feeling in the Level Three, that something that is needed in the space or by the people in the space. When these things are connected and the leader is oriented toward his or her Leader's Stake, leadership action becomes inevitable. In Emily's case, her own frustration, and her awareness of the growing frustration of the silent members of the group, became married with her urge to shift the group from contention and competition into silence and connection."

Stella pointed back to the model. "Which brings us around the diagram to ACT. So how and why does the leader act? These days, leaders often act for the glorification of their egos. Their Destructive Level One conversation wants to fix, control, or dominate the situation, with little concern for the Level Two (the needs and feelings of other individuals) or the group and space needs of the Level Three. Just as often, some leaders lay themselves out as a sacrifice to the people in their group: 'I'll take care of everything—

just stop fighting and be happy.' This is a false reaction to Level Three and is also completely dominated by destructive self–talk."

Zeke said, "When we admire really effective leaders, it's because they are usually marrying their urges and then stepping forward without knowing exactly what the outcome will be. So they aren't trying to over-control. And as effective leaders do step forward, they need to step forward with all editors off, giving all that they have, using their full range of abilities.

"When they do that, they will create an impact, sometimes intended and sometimes unintended. So, at the very time they step out with full permission, they need to be completely responsible for the impact of this full permission on the space and the people in it. They're stepping into a sort of paradox. Their editors have to be shut off, and yet they have to be completely conscious of what is happening so that they can shift and dance with the impact that they have on the people and the space that they are leading.

"Full Permission doesn't mean that the entire Destructive and Grounded Selves are dumped into the world just for the sake of that release. And Responsibility for Impact doesn't mean second-guessing everything that may occur so it will have the 'right' impact. Full Permission does mean that, from my Grounded, Level One Self, I will use everything in that self for the sake of the Stake. I will bring the full range of emotions and expression to the party, and I will step in with everything I have in every moment. For the sake of that Stake, nothing is held back.

"Responsibility for Impact means that I am responsive to everything that occurs from my actions. I'm conscious, I'm aware, and I take complete responsibility for whatever emerges from me as a result of those actions. When you put those things together, you are a leader in action, with all of what you have, taking complete responsibility for who you are and what you are doing."

Stella pointed to the diagram. "As we move around the model, the next word is *STAY*. You can see that it's on the model twice." Stella pointed to the space between *Responsibility/Full Permission* and *Awareness of Level Three*, and then to the space to the right of that, between *Awareness of Level Three* and *Urge*.

"That's because these two places are where leaders can easily get pulled off the model and hooked into that destructive Level One stuff. After you act with Full Permission and take Responsibility for Impact, what might occur is that you instantly judge the action you just took. You are sucked into a Level One pit. *Oh God! Somebody is upset with me! What did I just do?* Or you may receive judgment or strong reaction from one of the others you are trying to lead. Either of those can hook you, the leader, just like a fisherman hooks a fish. In those moments, you get yanked right out of leadership.

"The key is to *stay* with the impact that your action has on the space. You're already responsible for the impact; now you have to see how it lands, and for that to happen, you must *stay*. You must put your attention on the Level Three and see what is happening as a result of your action. You must stay with the group or the team instead of retreating into a private hell of self-criticism. You stay with whoever is having a reaction to you instead of judging them, moving away from them, defending yourself, or attacking them. Because you aren't hooked and because you are able to keep your attention on the nature of your impact on the Level Three, and because you realize that everything that is happening is through the lens of the Leader's Stake, you stay for the sake of that Stake."

Zeke stood up. "Okay, Unicorns. Now breathe. That was a lot, I know. We are almost all around the circle. This brings us to the top of the model: Awareness of the Level Three. Here's where *staying* really pays off. Hopefully, through your leadership or someone else's, the group is back on track. Now they are performing as needed; the goods are being manufactured, or the clients are being served, and the vision is being fulfilled. Now the leader retracts his or her antenna and lets the work progress. Emily did this last night. Once her work was done, she didn't need to keep running the show. She stepped back and let the group go on with the work it was formed to do.

"Until the next urge arrives and off you go again."

The first retreat was ending, and Emily knew that she had changed. As she was saying good-bye to the other members of the Unicorn Tribe, she felt that she had really connected with twenty-two people who might actually become friends.

But as she drove down the twisty coastal highway that would take her back to Pasadena, she realized that the change in her was even deeper. As long as she could remember, there had always been something inside her that she held in reserve: a private place where she could retreat and never be too hurt. She had spent a lot of time in her fortress of solitude since her separation.

Now, she could feel herself starting to come out of that self-imposed isolation. This first leadership retreat had helped her rediscover her own personal power, the courage to walk across that bridge. And from there, she had begun to be aware of her impact on others, mostly for better but sometimes for worse. More importantly, she was starting to care about other people, instead of working so hard just to protect herself. Wow! And Retreat Two was going to be about Creating from Other. She was almost ready to do that now.

Key Leadership Concepts in Retreat One

A **Leader** is one who is responsible for his or her world.

Leadership arises from an injunction, an inner knowing, a determination that impels you to take action. There is no leadership without a risk of failure. Each failure teaches something the leader needs to know. Skillful leaders in a conflict first seek to understand the other person's position.

Level One Awareness is the total focus of our attention on our internal monologue. It is a fascinated concentration on all our inner judgments, opinions, arguments, worries, lectures, daydreams, etc.

Level Two Awareness occurs when you open up and let the other person into your field of awareness. You are no longer focusing just on yourself. You are curious about and open to the other person.

Level Three Awareness is the ability to sense the space, the whole room, and all of the energies that are moving around in it. It is not just a sum of your noticing each person in the room. It includes the ability to read the emotional energies in a room, to sense what is going on in the space between everyone, rather than to know what is going on with just one or two people individually.

The Grounded Self is the face of Level One Awareness; it includes powerful thoughts, beliefs, opinions, attitudes, values, and purposes.

The Destructive Self includes the judgments, betrayals of self, justifications, excuses, and old stories that we tell ourselves over and over again. These negative diatribes seek to attack, limit, and constrict us. Our work on ourselves as leaders is to learn to feed the Grounded Self and to starve the Destructive Self.

Failure leads to success. Winston Churchill said, "Success is the ability to go from failure to failure without losing your enthusiasm." Each failure teaches something the leader needs to know. There is no leadership without risk, and there is no risk without failure.

Life Purpose is the meaning, purpose, and reason why you were born on this planet at this time, the work you were meant to do. Hopefully you will be tweaking, modifying, changing, and evolving your Life Purpose Statement for the rest of your life, as you grow and change. Discovering your purpose, your work in this lifetime, helps you craft your Leader's Stake.

The Co-Active® Leadership Model

A **Leader's Stake** is planted when a leader takes responsibility for an event that calls for his or her leadership. It is through these Stakes that your Life Purpose manifests in concrete projects leading to concrete change.

Stakes are not goals or outcomes. They are more foundational. Goals can be measured, achieved, and checked off on a to-do list. Goals serve the Stake.

Awareness of the Level Three: In any leadership moment, the leader is attuned to the needs of the group, the needs of the environment, his or her own needs, and the needs of the Stake. This is what we call Awareness of the Level Three.

Full Permission: You act with all of your being, not holding back, not being tentative, but fully impacting your world. It does not mean that the entire Destructive and Grounded Selves are dumped on the world just for the sake of that release. Full Permission means that, from your Grounded, Level One Self, you will use everything in you for the sake of the Stake.

Responsibility for Impact: Responsibility for Impact doesn't mean second-guessing everything that occurs so it will have the "right" impact. Responsibility for Impact means that you are "respondable" (i.e., responsive) to everything that occurs as a consequence of your actions. You are conscious, you are aware, and you take complete responsibility for whatever emerges from you. When you put those things together, you are a leader in action, with all of what you have, taking complete responsibility for who you are and what you are doing.

Stay means to focus your attention on the Level Three and see everything that is occurring as a result of your action. You stay with the group or the team instead of retreating into a private hell of self-criticism. You stay with whoever is having a reaction to you instead of judging them, moving away from them, defending yourself, or attacking them.

Co-Active Leadership is powerful because everyone is aligned around a common Stake. It is a Stake that the leader passionately holds, and it is compelling enough to ensure everyone else's participation.

Chapter Three

Journey into Vulnerability

Leadership cannot really be taught. It can only be learned.
Harold Geneen

"**I** didn't sign up for this!"

Emily was on the phone with her friend Victoria, complaining again.

"Hey, you never told me how much stuff happens in this leadership training between the retreats. Weekly pod calls, monthly tribe calls, book-reading calls, and enough homework to put me through graduate school. You never told me about this part!"

Victoria laughed. "Emily, you find the most interesting things to whine about. Let's see. Three months ago, you were whining that your life felt empty and that no one really cared if you lived or died. Now you are whining because there are twenty-two people who want to talk to you and you don't want to talk to them. Do you notice anything here?"

"All right, all right," Emily said. "Give me a break. I get your point. But really, what is it with all these calls?"

Victoria sighed. "Look inside yourself. Why are you having so many problems connecting with your tribe?"

This question opened up a can of worms for Emily, and she was still thinking about them long after she had hung up the phone. The last word in Victoria's request had been *tribe*. A tribe was a whole new concept for her. She knew how to relate to a client, a family, even a work group. But what, exactly, was a tribe? It seemed to be something more intimate than a random group of adults stuck together for a year. They weren't really friends yet, even though they might become friends.

Emily had lived in big cities all her life. She was totally comfortable with the relative anonymity that went with the urban environment. This "tribe" business had all the claustrophobia of a very small town. It made her feel exposed.

By asking her to look inside herself, Victoria had given her a real challenge. Emily knew that this problem of not wanting people to know her too well had much deeper roots than her just being a comfortably estranged city dweller. As she thought further, she began to see a long pattern of stepping away from relationships with people that might entangle her. She began to see more clearly this fear of being let down by others. Alongside that was a need to protect herself against disappointment that had set the tone for all her relationships. It probably had more than a little to do with why her marriage had fallen apart. Sure, it wasn't the only factor—her ex had made some really dumb choices. But she had to admit that her need for self-protection, and the walls she had built up between her and him, were definitely a major factor that had led to their breakup.

Maybe this self-protection was what her tribe members had seen during the spaceship exercise when they had called her cold and uninterested. And maybe it was part of what one of the other Beauty types had called "that thin membrane that separated me from others." She had a sick, sinking feeling as she saw how pervasive it was.

Then she remembered one of the sillier exercises in the retreat. Its point was to show how leaders need to ask for help and invite participation. She remembered feeling that she had failed miserably at that event. But she had learned an important lesson: that "strong leaders ask for help a lot." Maybe this would be a good time to practice.

The next morning, there was an all-tribe conference call. Emily brewed herself an extra-hearty cup of Irish Breakfast tea, settled into her overstuffed couch, put on her headset, and dialed in. Today she would ask for help.

But within ten minutes of the call, she felt as isolated as ever. Others checking in were fiercely alive, excited, and energized about how the leadership program was transforming their lives. Some of them seemed to be ignoring an agreement they had made at the beginning of the retreat—"I agree not to make any major life decisions for at least a month after each retreat"—and were already talking about blowing out of jobs and relationships, blazing with intention and commitment. Emily was feeling quite intimidated, especially by Allen, the Episcopalian minister.

"Hi, everybody," he said. "Guess what? I told my bishop that I'd had it! My Stake is to bring God's love into the world, and that is never going to happen as long as I'm just being an administrator. So I told him that I was ready to go back out in the field and preach, and that it was non-negotiable for me. He doesn't really like non-negotiable demands, so I don't know what will happen. I hope I don't get kicked out of the church. But I must do something! I won't live a lie anymore, or hide my light under a bushel. I am so grateful to this program."

In contrast with Allen's enthusiasm and intention, Emily's life didn't seem to have changed at all. And she certainly wasn't feeling all that grateful at that moment. In fact, she felt alone in her ambivalence and resistance. Then she thought about the leadership model. She became aware of a strong urge to speak up, not to ask for help but to address the fact that her experience was so different from what she was hearing on the call. And instead of defaulting to her usual cool, detached place and waiting until she had what she would say well planned out, she just jumped in.

"You know, okay . . . darn! This is Emily. I am not quite sure what I want to say, but here goes. I'm not having the same exciting experience as many of the rest of you. For me, a lot of the energy from the retreat is already fading. I'm noticing more and more resistance to all these tribe and book and pod calls. I am also seeing that this is an old pattern for me, of moving away from groups. Actually, I feel pretty shitty right now. Sorry."

"Thank goodness you spoke!" Emily was surprised. Isabel, her roommate during the retreat, had joined in. "Emily, I am struggling with exactly the same issues. I was feeling like a third armpit on this call until you spoke. I am not at all sure how to bring what we did in the retreat into my organization."

Phil Serrito, the corporate type whom she didn't like all that much, chimed in in agreement. "You know that rings true for me, too. I came back to work with the same messes waiting for me. This is the first call I have managed to make since the retreat ended. I was just too busy putting out fires at work."

A few others joined in, and for a while it seemed the tide had turned as people's stories of feeling stuck and confused proliferated.

Suddenly Allen jumped back in. "Okay, I get what many of you just shared. And I don't want to sit over here in righteous judgment—that's just junk that comes from my Destructive Self. So I'm not trying to make the folks who are struggling with this stuff wrong. I think it's hard for all of us to make big course corrections in our lives.

"But come on! What are we here to do in this lifetime? Go back to the same old rut? Keep on in the same old patterns that are comfortable in their normal, constricted familiarity? Or could we do something different, something amazing? I know you all read it, but listen again to this quote from Marianne Williamson in our leadership manual. Really listen, because I think it's easy to forget!

"Our deepest fear is not that we are inadequate. Our deepest fear is that we are powerful beyond measure. It is our light, not our darkness, that most frightens us. We ask ourselves, Who am I to be brilliant, gorgeous, talented, fabulous? Actually, who are you

not to be? You are a child of God. Your playing small does not serve the world. There is nothing enlightened about shrinking so that other people won't feel insecure around you. We are all meant to shine, as children do. We were born to make manifest the glory of God that is within us. It is not just in some of us; it is in everyone. And as we let our own light shine, we unconsciously give other people permission to do the same. As we are liberated from our own fear, our presence automatically liberates others.

"Sure, it's hard. But our work together is to step into our magnificence, not to settle for our comfort!"

It was quiet for a moment. Then Emily spoke up. "I hear you, Allen, and I agree. But I have to be honest about how hard it is for me to follow that path. I could easily take what Williamson wrote and turn it into another club to hit myself over the head with. My inner judge could easily chime in with, *See, Emily, you loser, you're playing small again!* So be patient with me, Allen. I'm definitely with you; I'm just marching at a slower pace."

Emily noticed the powerful impact her urge had on the tribe. She began to feel less like a stranger, more connected with the others. It touched her that by describing her own experience, she had started honest, open sharing about the range of different experiences people had as they tried to integrate this material. And by the end of the call, she felt closer to the tribe. As she put down the phone, she smiled at the paradox: sharing her isolation led to a stronger sense of community.

On her way home that evening, Emily discovered how all this Beauty-type stuff could literally be a lifesaver. She had an evening emergency intake at the women's shelter, and it ran very late. She was so wrapped up in the difficulties of the case that she forgot to ask for an escort to her car when she left the building to go home. She was within a few yards of her car when she heard footsteps running up behind her. She turned around. Just a few feet away, a tall, scruffy teenage boy skidded to a stop. He had dirty blond hair, and he was wearing a green Army surplus jacket, black pants, and designer sneakers. His hand was in his pocket.

"Give me your money *now*!" he yelled, his voice cracking a little.

It was odd. She wasn't scared. Mostly calm. Maybe because he had no weapon yet. A gun would have terrified her. As he started to lift his hand from his pocket, she just knew what to say.

"Don't worry, you won't have to pull out a weapon. I will give you all the money I have. My name is Emily. What is yours?"

"None of your fucking business!" The words were harsh, but his tone had quieted down. She reckoned he was just fifteen or sixteen years old.

"You look hungry. There's a café across the street. Can I buy you something to eat?" She didn't know where her calmness or this stuff she was saying was coming from. She was just acting on impulse, and her impulse was to be kind.

"No, you bitch! Just give me your wallet." He couldn't handle her kindness.

"Okay, I have to reach in my purse to get it. I can give you the credit cards, but they won't be much good once I call them in. It might be safer for you to stick to cash. I think I have around sixty dollars." He was sweating now. She felt sorry for him.

"Okay, sure, just give me the cash. And hurry!"

She handed over her wallet, and he took out the money and handed the wallet back.

She took out a business card and handed it to him. "I work in a women's shelter, and I have a lot of connections with homeless shelters, job programs, and rehab centers. If you ever need some help, just give me a call, and I can probably set you up with someone who can help you out."

Then he said, "Okay, uh . . . thanks, Emily. Bye." And he ran off.

She didn't know if she would ever hear from him again, but she marveled at how easily she could calm him down with her graceful, cool, blue Beauty energy.

The following afternoon, Emily got another reminder of how much she was actually changing. She had just finished talking on the phone with her last coaching client of the day and was heading to the kitchen for a celebratory glass of chablis, when the phone rang.

The voice of her ex-husband, Mike, on the other end was less than welcome. There was none of the usual "Hi, hello, how are you?" He just launched right in by saying, "Look, Emily, I want to talk about changing our divorce settlement. When we made our agreement, I said I would pay all of Francine's tuition through her undergraduate studies. But I just got another salary cut. I think it's only fair to renegotiate this payment. I need you to . . ."

She actually opened her mouth to blast him, and then she froze, her mouth still open, her knuckles white on the hand holding the receiver, her heart pounding. She asked herself a new question: *What is my Stake here?* She knew that she had been about to launch an attack based on an old Stake: "Make him take some responsibility for the chaos he created. Make him pay for being such a bastard!"

In fact, she had been operating from this Stake quite successfully for some time now, and it had been working quite well for her. She was very satisfied with the terms of the divorce settlement, and with the embarrassment her ex had suffered in court. But times had changed. That Stake didn't seem so compelling anymore. Actually, she could help out a little with Francine's tuition without suffering hardship. Maybe it was time to serve another Stake. What did she really want from him now?

She acted on her urge to be silent and to take her time, not just react. Mike was asking for a favor, and she wasn't compelled to grant it. After all, she had no Stake in continuing any kind of friendly relationship with him; she trusted him about as far as she could throw his nubile new sweetie. If she chose, she could just slam the metaphorical door in his face. And yet, while that might be momentarily satisfying, today it didn't have the draw it usually did for her.

In the prolonged silence, she felt her Beauty side come forward. She had all the space and time in the world. A coolness dampened her reactive fire and pointed her to a much more creative focus. What was her deepest truth in this moment? She stayed in this silence for what seemed to her to be a very long time, just mulling over this situation. Was there something else she wanted from him?

Sounding a little annoyed, her ex-husband asked, "Hey, Emily, are you still there?"

"Oh, yes, Mike," she replied, "I most certainly am. I'm thinking. Just give me a moment."

Then the new urge came, bringing relief and a bit of a surprise. She no longer needed to make him suffer. All she wanted was a little serenity, and one other thing. When they had divided their property, Mike had taken the Oriental rug that he had inherited from his grandmother. Emily loved that rug; in fact, she had given birth to Francine on it. When he'd rolled it up and driven off with it, she had felt one more deep, painful cut. She saw a new Stake emerge for her about this relationship: "Get what you need to end this relationship gracefully and without regret." Now she was ready to act.

"You know, Mike, I think we can work something out."

Chapter Four

Creating from Other

*If your actions inspire others to dream more, learn more,
do more, and become more, you are a leader.*

John Quincy Adams

"No, it's** not all right. Nothing's all right! It's not all right
that you take off every weekend and play golf while I
am stuck here with my belly so big I can't even tie my own shoes.
It's not okay for you to go running off to all your new tribemates
while I'm in my third trimester. And it's not okay bitching all the
time about Bill Sykes instead of listening to your wife when she
needs you." Melissa glared at him.

The sun was streaming into the kitchen, the birds were chirping
away outside, and Phil's morning had just gone all to hell. He
remembered seeing a poster at the center where they went for
Lamaze classes. It read: **CAUTION: Be good to your pregnant
wife so you'll live long enough to meet your baby**.

That was hard advice to implement right now. These days,
home felt like a war zone. According to his wife, so much of what
was wrong was "all your fault." If a man's home was his castle, then
every room in the house felt like a dungeon today.

"Look, Melissa, I'll cancel golf this weekend, okay? And I will think some more about dropping out of the leadership retreat." As she stomped out of the room without responding, he decided that she was correct. Nothing was "all right."

As he walked his Portuguese water dog, Diva, along the deserted, tree-lined streets of his neighborhood that afternoon, Phil finally made up his mind. It was time to quit that leadership program. It was ten days before the second retreat would begin. He had to face the hard reality that work and home were just too crazy. He couldn't just walk away from all that chaos for a mellow week in the woods.

And if home was a war zone, then work was a minefield. Any day now, he was going to step down hard on the one mine that would end his career. Phil was in charge of the West Coast division of his company. In a recent 360 evaluation, managers up and down the coast were almost one hundred percent behind his leadership, except for Bill Sykes. The conflict between them had played a major role in Phil's decision to take the leadership course in the first place.

CTI's Leadership Program had seemed like such a good idea back in October. He had confided his situation to his trusted golfing buddy, Sam, who had told him, in no uncertain terms, that he really needed to check out the program. And that first retreat had proved Sam right.

Phil had already begun using the language of Stake versus Goals with his managers. Almost all of them had actively participated in creating the Stake for the latest sales force recruiting drive: "Leaner, Meaner, and Greener. We attract the best young salespeople, and that drives us to number one!"

Most of them were now on board, but not Bill Sykes, the Southern California district manager and the bane of his existence. Bill was old-guard, a self-made guy who was a very close high school friend of Franklin Vesty, the company's CEO. Phil got along pretty well with Frank, but the congenial working relationship between Phil and his boss was nothing like Frank's long-term, intimate friendship with Sykes.

Phil wanted Bill Sykes fired. No hope. As long as Bill got adequate profits from his area, he wasn't going anywhere, and both of them knew it. Back East, corporate HQ had already told Phil to stop complaining about Bill and deal with it. Bill was from the Genghis Khan school of management. He treated everyone as an underling. Bill thought he should have been given Phil's job, and he let Phil know that on a regular basis.

All of that was manageable, but Phil had recently heard an unconfirmed but disturbing rumor that Sykes was courting their largest competitor and might jump ship, taking some huge accounts with him. If that happened, Phil would most likely get the blame, and the axe. And, to make life even worse, Sykes was becoming increasingly demanding and rude. "Hell, Sykes should be in the course, not me." Phil muttered. Fat chance! Anyway, with his job on the line, this was not an easy time to be disappearing off to the woods for a week.

Actually, right now, heading off into the woods seemed like a pretty attractive fantasy. Home, work—everything sucked right now. "Stop it," he told himself. He was just going to have to tough it out alone. If he could.

Next day, he actually lost it and slammed the phone on his desk after hanging up on Sykes's latest harangue. For a moment, he almost wished he could get himself fired. He'd worked so hard, and now it was all going to hell. And in recent weeks he kept asking himself, "For what?" Screw it. He was making more money than anyone in his family had ever imagined making. So what? The rumor of Sykes's imminent desertion just underlined his isolation in this chrome-and-leather prison.

He decided to send an email to Zeke, telling him about his decision to quit Leadership. An hour later, Zeke replied, asking him to call back after work that night. Phil really didn't want Zeke to run some sales job on him to keep him in the program. But what the hell—if Zeke was willing to talk to him after-hours, he felt he owed the guy at least a ten-minute conversation.

His wife was visiting her mother, thank God, and he had the whole evening to himself. He poured himself a glass of merlot, checked the clock to make sure he wouldn't miss the game that was starting in fifteen minutes, and made the call.

When he next looked at the clock, more than an hour had passed, his glass was empty, the game was forgotten, and he was still bitching about Sykes. It was actually great to have a sympathetic sounding board, someone who could listen to him rant about all the stress at work and at home without wanting to criticize or fix him. Then Zeke said something that was a game changer.

"Phil, you can come to the retreat or not, but there is one thing I will guarantee you. No, two things. One is that, in my opinion, the harder you keep doing what you are already doing with Sykes, the worse the situation is going to get. Remember back on the high ropes when Allen was on that platform and couldn't cross the rope bridge? No matter what he tried up there, it didn't work. Well, that is you right now. Doing more of what isn't working is never going to get you what you want. Einstein was right: insanity is just doing the same thing over and over again and expecting different results. Until you get unstuck from your own perspective about Sykes, nothing good is going to come your way.

"And I'll guarantee you one more thing. If you do come to this next retreat, by the time it's over, you'll see Sykes in a way you could never imagine from where you are sitting right now. Your relationship with him will change dramatically for the better, just from what you learn in this one week."

"Is that a money-back guarantee?" Phil asked.

Zeke laughed. "Sure, and I'll do you one better: I'll refund all fees you paid for the next three retreats, and I'll make you a side bet. Three hundred dollars says I'm right. I'll pay you if you tell me the second retreat didn't change anything in your relationship with Sykes. But if things do change dramatically in your life after Leadership, you'll donate five hundred dollars to the Leadership Scholarship Fund. Is it a bet?"

"Maybe. But the decision isn't really just up to me." Then Phil explained about his wife's mood in this last trimester.

Zeke didn't back down. "The retreat center is out of cell phone range, but we can make arrangements for you to call her every night. If she really needs you, you will be free to leave early. And who knows—I'm willing to parlay that bet and add to it that what you learn at this retreat will make a huge difference to your relationship with her, too."

That was just the push Phil needed. "Okay, you're on!" At least he would collect a fat check from Zeke and get a good meal out of it. Phil jotted down a note to make a reservation at the French Laundry, a four-star California restaurant, after the retreat. That might be a great way to reconnect with Melissa, even if the boys back East ended up firing him.

When he got to work the next morning, he found an email from Sykes that announced that he was taking a five-day vacation in Fiji, starting the following week. This news came totally out of the blue. Phil made a call to a trusted associate who worked with Sykes and confirmed that it was true. Sykes had been talking about it for weeks. He just hadn't gotten around to informing Phil. Well, at least that would give Phil some breathing room.

When Melissa heard he was leaving for the retreat after all, she just sighed. Oh well—at least it was better than a fight. Time to head for the woods and collect on a bet.

Phil had just finished folding the clothes from his suitcase and organizing them on the shelves on his side of the cabin when the door burst open.

"Well, looks like I'm going to be your roommate for this retreat."

Phil turned as Allen Bowers bounced in and made his announcement. Using his best professional smile, he said, "Great."

Phil cringed as Allen began to litter his belongings across his side of their tiny room. If there was one person at this retreat who was his complete opposite, it was Allen. Phil was trim, well dressed in business casual, neat, thoughtful, and moderate in all his habits. Allen was fat and messy, a minister, a (hopefully) ex-alcoholic, and one of those touchy-feely guys. And, even worse, Allen was so gung-ho about this leadership program, just like a damn Boy Scout!

Tucking an errant strand of white hair behind her ear, Stella opened the second retreat. "The last time we met, you discovered the world of leading by creating from self. In this retreat, we will be exploring creating from other.

"Relationships are at the center of everything we do as leaders. Yet so often, we try to be in relationship with the person who we think *should* be there that we don't even see the person who is actually in front of us. Being in relationship with another person involves intimacy. So an important part of this retreat is exploring what intimacy means, how it works, and how we use it in leadership. When we let go of our expectations and judgments about the other person and just get curious about who's over there in the other chair, we can actually create a relationship of intimacy, even if we have a history of conflict between us. Intimacy is fostered when we can stay connected around something larger than our disagreements or disappointments.

"We are in an interesting state in our world regarding intimacy. Most of us are longing for more closeness and connection in our lives. We yearn for it, and at the same time, we are afraid of it and distrustful of it.

"Intimacy got lumped in with sexual acting out and exploitation. So our culture has attempted to legislate, limit, and quantify the ways in which we can be in closer connection with each other. People may have acted with good intentions in the past, trying to protect victims of abuse of power. But that hasn't always worked so well. We've created so much confusion that, for many of us, intimacy at work has become a scary concept."

Zeke broke in, "Exactly. These days, we're instructed that it's actually inappropriate to have intimacy in many workplaces. I guess they mean sex. My sister, who teaches second grade, tells me that there are rules against intimacy between a student and a teacher. I think they mean that there can't be any hugging or touching at all! Even in kindergarten. Those poor, touch-starved kids."

Stella added, "*Webster*'s dictionary defines intimacy as the state of being intimate. Okay. At first glance, this seems to be completely unhelpful. However, after giving the matter some thought, I'm inclined to agree with *Webster* completely. Intimacy isn't an event or a thing. It's a state or condition that arises when we are able to be present with another. Intimacy is a condition that arises when we are able to be present with and aware of what is right here between us: what is present in the other, and what is present in us."

Zeke got out of his chair and paced across the front of the room.

"Intimacy can also be thought of as 'into-me-see.' I am not sure who coined this phrase or where I even heard it first, but it's brilliant in so many ways. And it can be misleading in some ways. In order for you to be able to see into me, I have to be able to remove all of the masks and other crap that I put on top of myself. I have to clear away all of the fog and confusion that I put between you and me. When I'm open and available for you to be able to truly see into me, then I'm available for intimacy. Even without this level of intimacy, I can still know you. I can be astonishingly effective at looking into you and exploring many of your facets. I can be very insightful about you. Nevertheless, no matter how great I am at getting my attention on you, until I can open myself and let your attention move past my armor and truly see me, we can't have intimacy." He was silent for a very long moment.

"Zeke's 'into-me-see,'" Stella continued, "inspires me to go out and establish the intimacy that I crave. But there is a dark side to it. It is easy to ignore your impact. You can be so narcissistic and self-involved that you think that the only work of intimacy is for you to let me see into you. 'I am so special—come and join me in looking into me!'

"If I can't get my own attention completely off of myself, and can't be completely over there, looking into you, I can't experience intimacy. I need both sides of intimacy, the capacity to really see the other person and the capacity to reveal my truest self to that person."

Stella paused, looking out at the group. Then she said, "I imagine at least one of you listening in is thinking, *So what? What's the big deal about intimacy?* Let me tell you: It's a *very* big deal! I think it's universal yearning. I believe that all humans crave intimacy at a very fundamental level.

"As you probably have guessed by now, I am not talking about sex, although we humans get mighty confused between the two. We'll talk more on that later. But right now I'm talking about a deeply felt connection with another person, a feeling of oneness together. I'm talking about the yearning to be seen and known by our fellow humans, and beyond that, to be known by the universe and by all of life."

Phil was feeling distinctly grumpy, muttering under his breath, "Oh, great! Just what I *don't* need—more New Age chatter." He hadn't come here to get all touchy-feely with a bunch of strangers. All this "into-me-see," universal-love BS was way too Southern California for him. He was here to see if he could find a way to manage a jerk and salvage his job. It brought him back to that terrible story night during Retreat One when everyone had dragged out all their dirty laundry. Too much information!

The next morning, Phil was still feeling resistant. As the sun streamed into the retreat room, he wished he could stream out of it, find a sports bar, and get a beer. Ignoring the leaders as they talked on and on, he spaced out and watched the blue jays squawking at each other on the branches outside the windows.

When break time finally arrived, Zeke and Stella asked everyone to find a quiet place outdoors and do a private ritual to free themselves from the thoughts, concerns, and pressures of their lives outside this retreat. They asked everyone to let go of distractions that could interfere with the learning process for this retreat.

Phil couldn't wait to get out of the room and walk alone in the woods. Ten minutes later, he was sitting on a mossy stump, looking out between the trees at the sunlit valley. He watched a squirrel circling around a tree next to him, chattering and scolding him for intruding into important rodent business. "Shut up!" he snapped. Mr. Squirrel was unimpressed with Phil's authority and kept on chattering. He decided to just ignore it.

He thought about his wife and how much he wished they could go back to the good old pre-pregnancy days. He remembered the camping trip when their Fiat had broken down in an isolated river valley. That was a great weekend! What had happened to the two of them since then?

The squirrel's incessant chattering intruded again. Phil took a deep breath and started to create an imaginary scenario where Sykes was actually apologizing to him for being such a jerk. He saw the contrite look on Sykes's face as he looked down, unable to meet Phil's eyes.

But that damn squirrel kept distracting him. All of a sudden, he thought, *What am I doing? I have a week away from you, Bill Sykes! I am not going to spend the whole time making up movies about you! To hell with this! Get out of my head!* Immediately, the squirrel leaped onto another tree and scurried off. The forest fell silent, and Phil noticed that it was a lot quieter inside his head.

Back in the meeting room, Phil had an unexpected urge to speak up. He knew that he wasn't about to start whining about his marriage. But he could talk about work. He announced to the whole group, "Things are tough for me right now. My wife is very pregnant, and I don't know how long I am going to have my job. There is a political situation at work that is about to blow up in my face. Since I drove into the retreat center, all I have been doing is thinking about how I can beat the guy responsible for it. It's killing me! It took a very annoying squirrel to wake me up. Look, I want to leave this whole mess with Bill Sykes back in the office and actually just be here. I want to find a way to—"

Zeke interrupted, "That's a great idea, Phil. Now let's make it into an action. Try saying 'I will,' rather than 'I want to.'"

Phil started: "Okay, I will leave . . ." Then he paused. How was he going to make this statement his own, and not just be a good, compliant student doing what Zeke asked him to do? He felt himself getting angry, both at Zeke, for interrupting him, and at Bill Sykes back home, for screwing up his life. And as he became aware of these thoughts, he saw the faces of his tribe mates in the room with him, watching him and clearly showing concern for what he was going through. What was his Stake here? Almost without conscious thought, it came into his mind: "I need to be a leader, not a victim."

His voice startled him, it was so loud. "Okay, Mr. William Sykes, get out of my head! You've tried enough to ruin my life. Leave me the hell alone this week, damn it!" In the silence of his mind, he added, *And, honey, I love you, but you leave me alone, too, just for now*. In that moment, something in his chest released, and he took the deepest breath he had taken in quite a while. He looked around at a circle of smiles. That felt good.

In the staff room that night, Stella handed Zeke a cup of herbal tea. "Hey, guy, what's going on? There's something in the Level Three today, and it's swirling around you. Where are you? What's the matter?"

Zeke looked up at her. "Nice catch. You're good. Yeah. I'm not one hundred percent here. My partner, Jason, moved out two nights ago, totally out of the blue. Just before I left to come here, he said that after five years together, he was sick of my running the relationship—that he felt like my servant. I'm trying to put it out of my head and just be present here. But I can't get over being pissed off. Why didn't he tell me sooner? And talk about bad timing. How could he do that, knowing I was heading right off to a retreat? And of course it would have to be the retreat on intimacy!

"I mean, I don't know. Maybe it wasn't so out of the blue. Maybe I just wasn't listening to what he'd been telling me. I do kind of run roughshod over everything and hear only what I want to hear. Shit."

Sitting next to Zeke on the overstuffed couch, Stella put her arm around his broad shoulders. "So that was why you were so quiet today. It must have been rough, talking about intimacy. I'm sorry. What do you need from me?"

Zeke coughed and then said, "How about a fast car and ten thousand dollars?"

Stella smiled. "No, Zeke, I don't want your eccentric answer. Really, what do you need?"

"I might need to lean on you. I may not be my usual showman self. I need you to step in like you did today when you see me get knocked off track. You picked it up and ran with it perfectly. I'm going to need more of that. It's going to be a long week."

Stella gave him a little punch on the arm. "Don't worry, partner. Raven's got your backside. I mean it. Take whatever space you need."

The next day, Phil couldn't do anything right. The tribe's first exercise looked simple: start clearing away the preconceptions and assumptions you have about other people. Zeke began by saying, "We put up so many walls, obstacles, and barriers between us and others that it gets very difficult to break them down. Behind those walls, we feel very alone and unknown and unseen. Intimacy requires that we start by creating a deep trust of ourselves. It demands that we begin to break down the walls. In order to do that, we have to create agreements with ourselves and with others that create an environment of trust and safety, so that we can begin to explore. One of the most powerful agreements we can make is to commit to clearing out the assumptions we make about each other.

"We humans are tireless assumption-generating machines. We make stuff up about everything that we bump into, especially other people. We observe some behavior in someone else that triggers an emotional reaction in us, and—boom—we make up something about them. This thing we make up could be an assumption, a belief, a projection, an opinion, a judgment, or a dozen or so other ways of seeing something as true. We are going to lump all those things together and call them assumptions for now."

Stella spoke up: "When I have an assumption about you, I'm no longer able to see you or know you. I can see or know you only through the veil of that assumption. The more assumptions I carry about you, the less I am able to truly know you or be curious about you, and the more I rely on all the stories that I have made up, stories that I am absolutely certain are true."

"Right," said Zeke, "and, as you can imagine, this is a major block to any kind of true connection, never mind intimacy. In Don Miguel Ruiz's book *The Four Agreements*, the second agreement is "make no assumptions." It's an agreement I've made with myself to live a cleaner and more conscious life that has deep connections and intimacy. However, I still find myself making assumptions—hopefully fewer and fewer as I evolve into my conscious maturity, yet I know that I'll still make them." He sighed dramatically. Everyone laughed.

Stella went on, "So, what do I need to do when I have an assumption that is getting in my way of truly seeing and knowing you? I need to be able to clear it. There are many ways to clear assumptions all by ourselves. One is just by being conscious of them. That begins to clear them. Writing them out and then doing some sort of clearing ritual can also help. You can also clear them by using a witness, a neutral partner. Sometimes you can even train the person you have assumptions about to be your witness. That is the 'World Series' of clearing assumptions. That can do some remarkable things to open up connection and intimacy. So, of course, today this is the high-bar exercise we are going to—"

"Yes," said Zeke, jumping up from his chair and taking over, "and there are some important protocols for clearing assumptions that need to be in effect to protect both the person clearing and the witness. First of all, no homicides. Just kidding. First of all, you must remember that it starts with you, the person clearing the assumption. You must be truly committed to clearing it; you must have a strong desire for a deeper connection with the person you have this assumption about. It can't just be another opportunity to throw more fuel on the fire of the assumption in order to strengthen it. There must be a real intention to clear the air between the two of you and get closer."

Zeke started his pacing again, moving faster and faster as he got into the topic. "Next, the person clearing the assumption needs to keep looking underneath it to get to their underlying beliefs, the core that's feeding the surface assumption or judgment that they're aware of."

"Sit down, Zeke," said Stella. "You're making us nervous." People laughed as he shrugged and sat back down. Stella went on, "Now, the witness's job is also important, and it requires excellent self-management. As the receiver of the assumption, you need to be absolutely committed to serving the person who's clearing the assumption. You serve the one who is holding on to this assumption so that they can *really* get clear of it. In order to do this, you need to be solid and grounded. You must avoid taking personally anything the other one says. You need to speak the following mantra silently in the back of your head: *This is not about me. I am here to serve this person so that they can get clear of this assumption.*"

Zeke added, "Don't ever forget this: Your job as the witness is *not* to coach or advise the person who has the assumption. Your job is just to listen deeply and 'feel' into whether or not the energy of the person doing the clearing is becoming clearer. You might ask a question or two to prompt the person into looking deeper or underneath, but do this sparingly. Mostly, you are just there to witness. And be sure to thank the person clearing for being so committed to the relationship and for creating more intimacy."

It seemed easy enough, but when Phil tried it, everything went south. He was working with Emily, the therapist. In the only tribe phone call that he had managed to attend, he had liked what she said about also having qualms about the program. But when he started doing this exercise with her, any connection they might have had just dissolved, and they were glaring at each other almost immediately. Suddenly Emily stood up and said, "Stop, right now! I need to get one of the leaders, because this feels rotten!"

Stella came over and began asking questions. "So, Phil, what assumption did you start out with?"

Phil answered, "Well, I told her that I didn't understand why, if she was a therapist, she let herself get so overweight."

Stella asked, "So, is it her weight, or your judgments and assumptions about her weight, that are interfering with your ability to communicate with her?"

Phil said, "No, it's not really either of those. I just thought she should take a look at it."

Emily began to splutter, and Stella had to stop her from interrupting. "Emily, I will give you room to speak, but let me finish with Phil first. Now, Phil, one of the things Zeke said about this process is that it's about clearing beliefs, not about trying to buttress your own assumptions or your own judgments. I really don't hear a desire on your part to get this belief out of the way of creating more intimacy between you. Rather, I'm hearing you continuing to judge her and regurgitate your stuff on her while you disguise it as feedback.

"Look, when we do that, we really make these things become the 'truth filter' through which we see each other. When I have an assumption that what I 'know' about you is true, I will see you only in that way. And it gets even worse if I decide that I need to tell you the 'truth' about you, a truth that I invented inside my head. I can't see the real you who is actually showing up here in front of me.

"I may look at you and say, 'Phil, you're nothing but a heartless, clueless corporate type with the sensitivity of a rock.' Then I go out and begin collecting information to support my opinion. As those assumptions start to stack up, the picture of you on my screen of 'truth' becomes something that may not resemble you in the slightest. And I am no longer seeing you at all, only my dark caricature of who I take you to be. Doesn't feel good, does it? But that's actually what you're doing with Emily.

"You've actually become unable to listen to Emily, or even be with her. You can only be with your assumptions about her, and all that you have 'created' her to be. So now try it again."

Shoot. Phil knew he was busted. Stella had caught him doing exactly that; he was just dumping his judgment on Emily. He felt very much on the spot right now, with both women looking at him, one curious and the other spitting nails. He took a deep breath. So what was the real truth here?

"Okay, so maybe I wasn't quite honest. I guess I was judging you. I have a thing about large women. My mother was fat—I mean, *really* fat. Nowadays, I guess they call people like her compulsive overeaters. I think I put some of my judgments about her onto you, because she never did understand her condition, and she died way too early from a heart attack. She's never going to meet her grandchild." As he told Emily that, he felt an annoying vulnerability welling up, and he pushed it back down.

"Oh, I'm so sorry," she said. "How long ago was that?"

Stella stopped her. "Emily, your job is to simply receive what he has to say, not to do therapy on it or interview him. Phil, you're not done yet. Now share the assumption you have with Emily for the sake of clearing it out of the way."

"Okay. I made the assumption that you were in denial about your weight, and now I can see that it's my crap, and not based on any actual experience I have of you."

Stella walked away. She wasn't needed here any more; at least, not for now. Phil hoped he was finally starting to get this right.

Phil's next failure came in the afternoon, when the tribe was outdoors in a meadow, doing a series of leading and following movement exercises adapted from actors' improvisational training. The exercises were pretty simple and, in Phil's estimation, rather pointless. That was, until he messed up.

He was partnered with Allen, his roommate. Phil was walking in one direction, and then when Allen approached, he was supposed to let Allen lead him into walking in another direction. But Allen was heading for a small ditch, clearly going the wrong way, so Phil needed to make a course correction. When Phil didn't meekly give in to Allen's new lead, they fell over each other and ended up on the ground.

Zeke came over to them as they lay there. As he helped them up, he said, "Don't worry about failing at this. You both played full out. Actually, you will get more from falling over each other than some of you would get by doing it perfectly. Your Stake was to get somewhere, and instead you landed on the ground. But as long as your overall objectives are clear, as long as your Stake is clear, you can always 'fail' your way toward your goal.

"In fact, the speed at which you move from failure to failure, and the amount of risk you are willing to take for the sake of your Stake, will determine your rate of progress. It's sort of like the way you steer a sailboat toward a destination. You're very rarely headed directly at that destination. Instead, you tack back and forth, back and forth. Each of those tacks is actually a small failure in going in the direction you actually want to go in, but you get there in the end. If I can see my failures more in that light, then every failure I experience is just an opportunity to learn and correct my course and find another tack. Now try again."

This time they nailed it. It became a dance for them, instead of just an exercise.

Back in the event room, Zeke laid out the context for what they had just experienced. "One of the most profound and life-changing ideas that we ever adopted at CTI is 'co-leadership.' Having two leaders together at the front of the room, equally responsible for what happens, and each of them entirely unique and powerful in his or her own right, creates amazing results. We discovered that some miraculous things occur when two leaders show up at one hundred percent.

"First of all, both of them are more likely to take risks and step outside of their comfort zone, because if things start to unravel, they know that they have a co-leader right there who will reel them in or step up to put things back on track. Secondly, there's an intimacy that's created with everyone in the room when two people are leading, taking risks, and, most importantly, free to be 'real,' rather than trying to look good or get it right. Lastly, when two people are responsible together for something, there is an accountability that tends to eliminate the 'cover your ass' and 'pointing the finger' syndromes."

"That's right," Stella added. "Just throw out the idea that it's a fifty-fifty partnership. There is something in that idea that suggests that if you perform fifty percent of the time, then you can coast the other fifty percent and your partner will pick up the slack. All kinds of beliefs spin out from that, such as 'Don't take up too much space, and be sure to give your partner half of the airtime.'"

Zeke continued, "There's plenty of room for both leaders to bring one hundred percent of themselves one hundred percent of the time. So we think of the leadership dance as—"

"One hundred percent—one hundred percent, not fifty-fifty." Zeke smiled as Stella broke in. "This also means that co-leaders will not always agree, nor are they always moving at the same pace, or in the same direction, as each other. That's just fine, because you are not alone. Sometimes things can get sloppy, interruptions can happen, and failures and recoveries are guaranteed. Your goal as a leader is not to fit smoothly against your co-leader's shape, and it's not to avoid stepping on his or her toes. It's not to blend together perfectly all the time, never making waves. No, your goal as a co-leader is to play full out, to love that your co-leader is also playing full out, and for both of you to serve your shared Stake.

"To begin the dance of co-leadership, each leader needs to be completely present in his or her own power and in this present moment in time. Each leader needs to be open to input from his or her co-leader and from his or her environment. Each leader needs to be flexible and able to adjust quickly in response to those inputs. When that flexibility is present, a fluidity develops where the co-leaders find themselves finishing each other's sentences. They begin to listen, not just to what their co-leader is saying, but to what she's *not* saying, and then they flow with that as well.

"When each leader is one hundred percent present, open, and flexible, and both are aligned with their Leader's Stake, all sorts of disagreements, differences, and points of view can coexist, and the co-leaders can dance with them. What begins to happen is that the differences between them are respected, yet at the same time, these differences don't take control of the relationship and the nature of what is being led. What determines the leadership is the Leader's Stake and the co-leaders' ability to be present, open, and flexible with what shows up when that Stake is clearly and powerfully held."

"Absolutely," said Zeke. "And there are a few skills that we need to work on to make this dance of co-leadership work. The first one is a great tool we have adapted from the world of improv comedy; it's called 'Yes . . . And.' In improv, you're trained to say yes to everything that's thrown at you, to accept it, to acknowledge it, and then to add to it with the 'and.' In order to do this, you have to be grounded in yourself and be able to listen to what your co-leader is saying. Even if you have a different opinion, you create from it, blend with it, and then move with it."

Stella continued, "Yes, once you move with that blending 'yes' action, your co-leader will feel met—"

"And he or she will now be able to move with you in the direction you want to take." Zeke finished what she was saying.

As the class started to laugh, Stella came back. "Your co-leader will feel met. And when he or she blends with you, you'll also feel met and seen. And it goes on like this, with each one taking it forward while the other goes with it. It's an elegant and continuing dance of blending and leading, blending and leading, that allows the leadership to be authentic and shared. Out there in the meadow today, many of you experienced that dance and enjoyed it."

Stella went on, "But there are times when 'Blend and Lead' isn't the right strategy. Perhaps your co-leader has lost his or her connection with the Leader's Stake, or may even be taking things over a cliff. That's no time to blend. Saying 'yes . . . and' just won't cut it. In one of these rare moments, you 'break' into what is going on and your partner 'gives' leadership over to you. In this 'Break and Give,' it's necessary for the two of you, ahead of time, to have a clearly designed alliance built on trust, and to know that breaking and giving will occasionally happen. The partner who is doing the breaking stops the action and, with confidence, certainty, and clarity, takes it in another direction. The partner who was 'broken' immediately gives full power and permission to his or her co-leader and moves in the direction that the other co-leader is moving in, without attachment to any prior direction. This requires that both of you have absolute trust in each other.

"You all got to experience the physical movement of both 'Blend and Lead' and 'Break and Give' today. For some of you, it was easy. For others, it appeared to be a bit of a struggle."

Zeke laughed. "Right, Phil? As you and Allen discovered, this means that ego and attachment don't have any room to exist in this dance. Now, it's very possible that co-leaders will want to get together later to talk about what happened. They may even still disagree at that later time and need to work that out. That certainly happens between Stella and me sometimes."

Stella started to laugh. "Believe me," she said, "it's more than just sometimes. We're both strong leaders, so our dance can be more like an intense tango, not at all sedate."

"The important thing here," added Zeke, "is that the combination of trust and connection with our Leader's Stake and with each other is always greater than any need to decide who's right or wrong."

Stella continued, "Something really important needs to happen for this dance to work: it's letting go of ego, of the need to look good, and of the need to always get it right. In order for me to give all that up, I need to have two things firmly in place. First, I need to have a powerful Leader's Stake that I know that my co-leader and I are completely aligned on. Second, I need to trust that my co-leader will be there when I mess up, and that he or she will come in and save my butt.

"My co-leader also needs to know that I am there to save his butt when things go south or mess up in some way. He knows that I will blend in and move the focus back toward the Stake."

Zeke made a point: "Like, right now, I am taking over the focus from Stella because I'm sensing that this is all too abstract. So I'll talk about how it applies to Stella and me. We can get caught in our familiar traps. For example, I can get caught by the lure of a juicy idea and the intellectual riff that goes along with it. I can get so caught up in the exploration of the idea that I lose connection with the room and with our shared Stake.

"And my co-leader might get caught in the trap of relationship and taking care of people, and lose the point that needs to be made with the entire room in relationship with the Stake. Hey, traps like these have already happened between Stella and me in this retreat. But it's no big deal. She's so connected with our dance that she blends right in and moves the conversation or work in the direction it needs to move in. It's really a brilliant model."

Stella smiled. "He said with so much humility."

"I meant the strategy is brilliant, not us. Although we are," he replied.

"Like I said, humility. But Zeke's right. The thrilling part of the dance is that it's so far away from the boring lecture style and gets us into this place that's brand new every time, all the time. It's always a completely unknown adventure, because I'm meeting you in a space that is not just you and not just me; it's a blend of both of us, much larger than the sum of the parts."

"You have a taste of this right now," Zeke added. "Don't worry if you don't quite follow every word I said. After you do the high ropes work tomorrow, these concepts will be rooted deep in your bones. You won't come back from tomorrow's experiences the same person—that, I promise you." And with that, Zeke looked straight at Phil and smiled.

That evening, before dinner, the tribe was told about an assignment that they would be expected to complete within the next two months. They would create and co-lead some sort of public event with another tribe member. At first, Phil could not decide whom he wanted to work with. He knew it wasn't Allen or Emily but had no idea who it might be. This was unusual for him, as he knew he was usually very decisive.

As he stood there, debating with himself, Isabel came up to him. She wasn't even remotely on his list of potential candidates. "Be my partner," she said directly. "I don't want one of these New Age types. You at least know the world I work in." For Phil, that was an irresistible invitation, and he agreed. Isabel told him that her center had an event coming up called Gratitude Month. Over dinner, they began planning a simple event that would focus on teaching about the power of acknowledgment and gratitude. Although Phil wasn't totally comfortable with it, he found that he already liked working with Isabel and felt it could turn out to be a very positive experience.

When Phil called home that night, he got the answering machine. Feeling guilty at how relieved he was, he left a brief message and then hung up. The retreat phone was located near an old Mac computer, so he went online to check his email. He scanned the subject lines until he found what he hoped for: *All's well on the Western Front.* This was a signal from Saul, his executive administrator, who was holding down the fort at work. It meant there were no emergencies for him to be concerned about.

He logged off and wandered into the fireplace room, where he could see the other participants chatting away in groups of two or three at small tables or on couches near the fireplace. He walked over to the tall windows and looked out to see Olivia laughing with a group in the hot tub. Allen and Emily were in an intense dyad on the bench overlooking the valley, awash in a pearly glow as the silver moon lit up the incoming mist.

Phil didn't feel like breaking into any group. He was alone, too alone. At work he had made it to the top of the heap, and now, suddenly, he felt cut off from the people he led. They were actually getting along without him! At home he was distant and edgy with his wife. And he had no real friends, just superficial golf buddies.

At four in the morning, Phil was wide awake, listening to Allen's soft snoring. It wasn't the noise that was keeping him awake. His busy mind kept chewing. Intimacy—ha! What a joke. He had no one to be intimate with. Through a small window over his bed, he watched the clouds move past and then turn pearly as they swept across the full moon.

The tribe huddled together in raincoats under the tall redwoods, looking for drier places to stand. From time to time, a large drop would find its way past Phil's collar and down the back of his neck. They were doing more exercises on the high ropes. Phil didn't mind stepping out into any situation alone. He was pretty fearless in that regard. But this time, he was going to have to take responsibility for a partner, too. Phil was also harboring a secret. He had a fear of heights. He managed it perfectly in the first retreat by looking straight ahead or upward, never down. But today he was going to have to rely on someone else. He was going to have to tell them about his acrophobia. He'd need someone strong to pick up the slack. Damn. In his head, he started making a list of weak partners in the tribe whom he hoped he wouldn't have to climb with.

While Zeke was climbing the hill to set up the video camera, Stella laid down the context for the day's events. "In the first retreat, we learned how to create from self. And while there's absolutely nothing wrong with creating from self, it does limit your resources. Even if I am doing something with you, if I am just creating from self, my focus is inward and it's hard to truly see you, know you, be curious about you, or learn from you.

"Today you are going to get 'in your bones' what we mean by creating *from* other. We are used to creating *with* other people. Those relationships look like this: Side by side with another, I go through life; I brainstorm, collaborate, and create projects with this or that other person. In an ideal side-by-side 'with' relationship, I bring fifty percent and you bring fifty percent. In reality, one person usually brings some percentage greater or less than that fifty percent, and the other person balances it out.

"Creating *from* other means I turn to face you. Then I focus my full attention on seeing and knowing you, and on opening myself up to be seen and known by you. When I include you and see into you, I am in a position to go beyond merely creating 'with' you. I now have this entire other resource opened up to me. I can create 'from' you, and you can create 'from' me. We now are able to be present with each other, and each of us contributes one hundred percent of ourselves to whatever endeavor we are engaged in together.

"This simple shift of focus from fifty-fifty to one hundred percent–one hundred percent opens up a completely new, powerful, and potent world. It opens me up to learning how to listen deeply to you and to feel profoundly heard by you. It allows you to be completely you and me to be completely me, and it brings the possibility that we will see, know, and create from our complete beings. This is why we put so much emphasis on intimacy and the ability to connect deeply with another. When we can do that, we can create from another and access so much more of both of us."

Phil put on his harness and found himself standing in front of his partner, Olivia, the number-one person on his list of Phil's Least-Wanted Partners. He wanted to go back to his warm bed. In the first retreat, Olivia had been another of the people who had frozen when they tried to make their first climb. She had ended up calling for the instructor to come up and get her, utterly failing at the event. He could still see her up there, whimpering for help.

Zeke was back down with the group. He scraped a clod of mud from his irreparably dirty jeans and said, "All right, now, you two, just breathe and look into each other's eyes while I speak to you. This time, you won't be alone up there. You have someone you can rely on and who is relying on you. This gives you access to parts of yourself you may never have known you had. Just be aware of whatever anxiety you have, and let it drain out as you look at your partner's eyes. The two of you can do things together that neither of you might be able to do alone. Now say whatever you need to say to each other, and then climb on."

Phil wasn't about to tell her about his fear. She was too weak, and the event would be doomed from the start. He smiled and said, "Olivia, I am completely not afraid of this event. Use my strength. Know I have your backside all the way."

Olivia said, "Okay, I am really glad to hear that. I am still scared shitless, not to mention soaked and freezing, but knowing you are not afraid helps. I will hold up my end, even if I am ready to run. Let's go up!"

Phil climbed up the tree first and waited on the small platform for Olivia. Okay, so he hadn't been completely honest. Although he had no fear of climbing or of going out on the wire, he did get mild vertigo when he had to look down, which made him a little dizzy. But Olivia didn't need to know that—she was scared enough as it was. And luckily, this event was all about looking at each other, not down at the ground.

He watched impatiently as Olivia slowly climbed toward him. The ladder wobbled slightly against the trunk of the tree as she ascended, and she froze for a moment. *Oh no*, he thought. *Is it ending already?* He called out to her, "Olivia, you're almost up here. Come on, I'm getting lonely." She laughed weakly, but she started climbing again.

Phil looked out over the treetops at the falling rain and planned his strategy. In order to succeed in this event, they were going to have to lean into each other as they moved along the wires. Olivia was much too small to be able to support his weight. So he would have to hold her up while urging her to keep her back straight. Even if they were able to leave the side of the tree, he doubted they would be capable of taking more than a step or two. He wished he had gotten to do this with one of the more athletic people in the tribe. Oh well.

Olivia finally made it up to where he was standing and turned to face him. "Hi, Olivia. Welcome to *our* platform. Are you okay? Is that rain, or are you sweating?"

"I hate these things," she said. "Just a little scared of heights, that's all. Actually, not a little, but I am not going to let it stop me this time."

Phil wiped the rain off his right hand and then took Olivia's outstretched wrist. She didn't look like she could let go of the tree with her left hand. He said confidently, "Let's try it." Then he reached out, took both her small hands, and almost pulled her off the wire. They both let go and grabbed for the tree, barely catching themselves. "What was that about? You nearly yanked me off of there!" she said.

"I was just trying to hold you up and support you."

Olivia laughed nervously. "Thanks. With that kind of support, we'll be on the ground in no time. You don't trust that I can hold your weight, do you?"

Phil was busted once again. "Uh . . . well . . . I'm just trying to help. But . . . well . . . no, you're right. I don't really think you can hold me up."

Olivia was getting pissed. "Look, you may be right or you may be dead wrong, but you will never know by trying to do it all. So stop helping! Look at me. No, really, look right into my eyes. I'm here. Stop thinking about anything else and just look at me."

He looked at her. She had the biggest, bluest eyes he had ever seen. They were flashing at him right now. They took each other's hands again. They were standing there, balancing on their individual wire by holding on to each other. Instead of thinking about how he was going to fix the situation, Phil just looked at her. She was rock solid, and it was actually *his* body that was trembling a little. Then Olivia gave a wiggle of her hips and laughed.

Zeke's commanding voice came echoing up to them. "Okay, you two, now start moving your feet sidewise and move out on your wire. Go slow, and keep leaning into each other."

"Let's go, big boy." Phil could feel Olivia's strength and confidence flow into him. He had a brief image of how shy and quiet she had been on that first day, and how she had cried when she had been voted to be burned up by the sun. What a shift! She was so a Sex type!

With her urging, he began to move. Then he almost toppled the two of them. They were off balance, so he went back to his old strategy and decided he needed to step in and hold them both up. Big mistake! Luckily, he heard Olivia shout, "No, Phil, don't straighten up. Stop trying to hold me up! Lean into me. I can take your weight—just lean in! Now look at me!"

He looked back into her eyes. *Whew, that was close.* He leaned in even farther. She had him solidly supported. The more he leaned on her, and the more she leaned on him, the more stable they became. So this was what they meant by creating *from* other. Hey, this was actually kind of fun.

Time slowed down. The rain no longer mattered. It was just the two of them, and they were moving in rhythm. It was delicious. Finally they tumbled, laughing and still holding hands as they went over, having gone much farther out on those wires than he'd ever thought possible.

Back down on the ground, Olivia received a big hug from Zeke, almost disappearing in his enormous arms. Then he did the same thing with Phil. When Zeke finished the hugs, he said, "Phil, you did good up there. You really trusted her." Phil looked away. He didn't want Zeke to see how much those words meant to him.

It was the final event that gave Phil his most profound insight into the power of creating from other. This exercise was a little more complex. The two of them had to edge out on a wire running between two trees. A few ropes hung down for them to grab for support, like straps on the subway. But the gaps between these ropes were wide, and they couldn't move from one to the next unless they remained hand in hand.

This time, Phil and Isabel were paired up, because they would be working together on their assignment between the second and the third retreat. For this event, the added twist was that while they were edging along on the wire, they were to tell the other tribe mates, far below them on the ground, something about their future project.

This time, Phil's partner seemed fearless from the start, and he wasn't scared of moving out onto the rope either. But he noticed that his stomach twisted a little at the idea of standing up there, looking down to talk to the audience far below. Pesky acrophobia! He didn't keep that information a secret this time. If there was one thing he had learned from his event with Olivia, it was that when he tried to be a superhero, he messed everything up. He needed to be straight from the start about his fear. As they planned their strategy on the tree, he said, "Hey, I'm not afraid of the wire. It's just when I look down, I can get a little dizzy and tense."

She said, "Okay, no problem. Look, I'm completely comfortable up here. Let me go out first and get the first hanging rope; then I'll come back and get you."

Then Phil surprised himself.

"No, that isn't going to change anything. I need to do something about this fear. Let me go out first and start the talk."

Isabel smiled. "I love that. So what do you say about both of us going out together? We stand or we fall as a team."

They high-fived and headed out, Phil in the lead, Isabel right behind him. It seemed to Phil that he just glided to the first hanging rope. And then to the second one. With each of them holding onto a rope, he looked down at the other people on the ground below them. The dizziness started rising up. Then he felt Isabel's firm hand in his. She gave him a little squeeze of support. He took a deep breath, swallowed hard, and started speaking.

"Our presentation is about gratitude. Right now I am really grateful for two things. I am grateful that the wind died down. And I am grateful to be up here with my partner, Isabel. Look how rock-solid steady she is. We may get to the other side of this wire or we may fall, but we are a team."

As he headed out to the next hanging rope, Isabel spoke while she moved, "Gratitude. You know how to say that in Spanish? *Gratitud*. We pronounce it a little differently, but it is the same word. *Agradecimiento*, appreciation for this moment, and for all that has brought us to this moment. When we are stuck, when we are paralyzed, even for a moment; when you're like Phil and me, arguing about who was going to go out on the wire first; when decisions and fears immobilize us—these are the times to bring in gratitude. Gratitude lifts you out of all that and into a place where all the petty anxieties and squabbles start to dissolve. And then you can go on, like Phil and I need to do right now."

Suddenly, the wind came back with a vengeance and the whole height-dizziness thing hit Phil hard. He grabbed tightly to a hanging rope with one hand, and Isabel's hand with the other. He turned and looked at her. He had to do something, or he was just going to give up and fall.

He said the first thing that popped into his head: "Honey, could you go get me a cup of coffee?"

She laughed and answered, "Shut up, wiseass, and get moving." Then she stunned him. Letting go of his hand, she reached over and wiped a raindrop off his nose. Then she simply placed her hand on her own waist and said, "Go finish this thing for us."

Phil suddenly relaxed. He didn't have to be alone, trying to look brave, trying to do it all himself. He had a partner who was unafraid, who liked him and who trusted him enough to let go and let him recover his balance. No matter what happened next, it was all okay. He was ready to take another step on the wire. This was easy. He was amazed to discover that they were only a couple of feet away from the ending platform.

He spoke as he inched his way toward the platform. His words surprised him. "And the one thing I am most grateful about is that I don't have to do everything alone anymore. I have been fighting the good fight all my life, but as a man on my own. What could I do if I joined with another person, or ten other people, and do what I needed to do? What if I could lean in and they could lean in? There's nothing we couldn't accomplish!"

As he finished this speech, he grabbed on to the tree on the other end of the wire, with Isabel right behind him. They had made it, together. Righteous! The cheers came from their audience as they hugged.

That night, Phil called home again to check in with Melissa. He was so excited about what had happened on the high ropes as he launched into his story.

". . . and then I had to give a lecture to the whole group while I was on a wire fifty feet above the ground. My partner, Isabel, wanted to go first . . ."

Eventually, he became aware of the absolute silence on the other end of the line. "Honey, am I just blathering on? I'm sorry."

She said, "No. That's fine." He heard the flatness in her tone.

"How are you doing?" he asked.

"I'm glad you're having a good time. And to tell you the truth, Phil, it's actually easier without you around."

He tried not to show how much that hurt. "Look, it's late," he said, "and you're probably pretty tired. Let's call it a day, and I will tell you more when I get back home."

"Okay, goodnight, then." And she hung up.

The next morning, the tribe gathered in a large circle in the meeting room to debrief the ropes events. Zeke started. "Phil, tell us what happened when you were on that tree for the final event. It seemed like you just walked out on that wire quite fearlessly."

Phil laughed. "Yeah, if you weren't looking at the wet spot on my shorts. No, I wasn't scared of walking out there. But I really didn't like the looking down. See, I have vertigo when I look down, so I knew that if I had to lecture to you all down there, I would go over. But I talked about it with Isabel, and that helped. Especially when we joked together. We were a team, so I stopped worrying about it."

Stella noticed something in his face as he spoke. "Phil, I am guessing there is something else you want to say."

"Yeah. Something happened up there that I don't really understand. Isabel was planning to go first, and I thought we might get halfway. Then I said I wanted to go first, and I could still see us falling. But then Isabel said, 'Let's go together.' Well, first, I never thought of that. But all of a sudden, I just knew that if we did that, somehow we would make it across the wire. And I kind of dreaded looking down to talk, but when I did, I felt this enthusiasm and support coming up from the people below me, and it made me steadier."

Isabel started laughing. "Hey, mister, you practically dragged me across that wire. You talk about me being steady? You were a train engine; I was just the caboose."

Stella looked at Zeke, who nodded. Stella said, "Yes, I guess it's the perfect time to introduce a new word to your leadership vocabulary: *sourcing*. Every river has a source. Most rivers actually have many sources, many streams and tributaries that feed the river in its journey to the sea. Isabel was a source for you up in that tree.

"What if you could be the source of someone else's success or failure? What if, like that river, you were one of the many sources that fed another person's chance to produce amazing things in their life? My belief is that we are always 'sourcing' each other, usually unconsciously. I believe that once you're able to create a strong Level Two connection with someone, then you can consciously be a source of their success. You can focus your attention on what they're doing, the risks they're taking, and the moves they're making. Then you can be the source of their finding the extra inch or the extra ounce of energy they need to get across that last gap.

"I've seen it over and over again. A person reaches what he thinks is his limit, that point where he says, 'I can't go any further!' and someone else, or a group of people, is there, seeing past that limitation and seeing him go further than he ever imagined. Sure enough, that person takes another step or leaps into some new and unknown place, because that person or those people knew that he could and actually 'sourced' him into going further. Later on, this new, stronger, and larger person looks back and says, 'It was a miracle' or, 'I have never felt so loved.' That is the power of sourcing."

Phil nodded. This creating-from-other stuff was actually starting to make sense. Together they had done something that he had already decided was impossible. But by sourcing the strength and belief that the two of them had together, and by feeling the strength and support coming from the other members of his tribe on the ground, cheering him on, he had done something that he felt was almost miraculous.

He remembered back to almost three years earlier. He'd been in a disastrous work group where no one had anyone's backside. He'd seen them make catastrophic decisions because everyone was afraid of rocking the boat. The only thing that group had sourced was stress. If Isabel had been in that group with him back then, the outcome would have been so different.

Zeke turned the focus to Olivia. "We know that many of our fears are merely constructed beliefs, negative Level One conversations that keep recycling in our mind. Olivia, remember when you first panicked on the ladder when we were doing the high-ropes events during our last retreat? You froze, and then you found some inner strength, recovered, and took another step. You began that conversation all over again, and through that process got up the tree and actually onto the platform, further than you ever imagined was possible."

"I know," she said. "But then I messed up again. I just got too tired or scared or something. It was just too much for me. It's just like everything—"

Zeke interrupted her. "Yes, the conversation and the recovery over and over again *were* exhausting, and you had to ask for help to come back down. You made a powerful choice, having to overcome your fear over and over again. When you came down, you were celebrated and acknowledged for stepping through your fear and recovering to your power, and yet you were disappointed with yourself. You knew you had enough physical strength to go all the way across the bridge. But it was that inner conversation of mastering the fear that exhausted you, not the climb up the ladder. You really want to be able to rid yourself of that inner conversation, and not just in climbing trees, either!"

"God, that's the truth!" she said.

Stella joined in. "So, let's talk about yesterday's first event. There you were on another high ropes course where you were going to have to climb tall trees. The conversation about fear of heights started all over in your mind, and you were beginning to tire yourself out on the bus on the way to the ropes course. Only yesterday was different; yesterday your job was to find the power in connection and intimacy. Yesterday, instead of recovering to your own strength and power, your job was to find the connection with your partner and recover to that. You showed up so very differently this time!"

Then Zeke turned to Phil. "You zipped over the high-ropes events in the first retreat. But you almost failed in the first moments of the first event today. How did you recover? What helped when you were doing the first event with Olivia?"

Phil said, "I stopped being the expert and listened to my partner. I looked into Olivia's eyes. I stopped trying to help her and just leaned in on her."

Zeke smiled. "Right! You looked at Olivia and actually asked for help yourself. Your partner demanded that you look into her eyes and connect. You felt that connection deep down in your center, and you used that connection and your partner's faith and belief in you to go out on that wire. The need to control the situation wasn't even present; what was present was that deep connection."

Phil interrupted, "Well, I can't say the desire to control wasn't present at all!" Everyone laughed as Zeke continued, "Yes, but that wasn't what was driving you. You were up there on the wires, facing your partner. You were whispering to each other, and the connection was deep and so palpable that those of us watching from the ground could feel its power and its beauty. Then what happened?"

Phil said, "Twice, I nearly toppled us over trying to hold her up. My old 'do it all' routine. She called me on it and got me to just lean in instead of doing everything. It worked!"

Stella sat up in her chair. "Yes! You found your strength in your partner. You stepped forward with your heart to serve both her and yourself in moving out on the wire and completing the event victoriously. I am willing to bet that in that moment of connection, bombs could have gone off and sirens could have sounded and wasps could have buzzed around you, and it would have all been just noise in the distance. It wouldn't have fazed either of you, because the unity and synergy of that connection were more powerful than either of you could imagine. And you may not have noticed it, but the two of you went out farther on those wires than almost any other pair.

"You discovered the 'co' in *co-active*, that power of relationship and connection to move you through fears and old stories and limiting beliefs. Imagine what you can do from that place. Now you can collaborate, create, and lead fearlessly. You can break free of old patterns and boxed-in ways of doing things and venture in risky new directions.

"And you can do these things because you are held by that connection with your co-leader. You know that someone has your back and knows your strength. You know someone is there to serve that something that is greater than either one of you."

The dining room was particularly noisy that night. Phil held his dinner tray tightly as he scanned the room, looking for the person he wanted to talk with. There she was, with an empty chair next to her. He was in luck!

As he dissected his Cornish game hen, he said to Stella, "I feel very close to the two women I was on the ropes with today. I mean, almost closer than I do to my wife. This feels weird, and I don't like it too much. What's going on?"

Stella grabbed a pen and drew a triangle on the paper tablecloth. "Yes, that makes perfect sense. To understand what is going on for you, we need to look at the current, sorry state of the world today." At that point, both Isabel and Allen pulled their chairs around to see what Stella was drawing. At one point of the triangle, she wrote *Power*, and at another, she wrote *Sex*. At the third point, she wrote *Intimacy*.

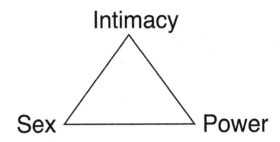

"So much suffering in relationships at work and in our lives comes from ignorance about the principles that are expressed in this triangle of intimacy, sex, and power. And yet I believe that a refined understanding of intimacy can change the world and transform the way we humans relate to one another."

She pointed to the diagram she had drawn: "There are three lines connecting three distinctly separate aspects of the human experience. We often confuse these aspects. We mistake sex for intimacy, we seek power through sex, and we confuse power with intimacy. And then, from a fear that we are going to make big messes in our lives, we make one of two basic life-destroying choices: either we shut ourselves off from life by creating insurmountable boundaries around our experiences of intimacy, sex, and power, or we lose our boundaries between them and get confused about where one begins and the other ends."

As she was talking, Olivia and Emily joined the group. Emily had her arm around Olivia's shoulder. Isabel leaned over from the other side of the table.

"That is so true!" said Isabel. "It's even worse for a woman in power. There is so much crap that gets projected onto you. I have to hold myself back from simple affection because I am afraid of how it will be interpreted or how it looks to someone observing me. At work, I don't dare show the kind of affection Olivia and Emily are showing right now."

"Yes, there is a ton of focus in our society on the sex-power axis in this triangle," Stella said. "All of you who make it to this program have self-mastery skills in that area, so I'm not going to focus too much on that axis. The whole sex-power conversation is actually quite common and seems to be spread all over the news for our entertainment almost every day. It isn't at all entertaining for those people who are caught up in messed-up boundaries and confused definitions. That's probably a whole retreat in and of itself.

"But in this model, I want to look primarily at the confusion that exists on the intimacy-sex axis and on the line connecting Intimacy and Power.

"Today, on those high ropes, you experienced intimacy and connection with another. As we begin to let ourselves feel the attraction of that intimacy, what often happens is that we get all confused, thinking this is about sexual attraction and that the eventual end of this intimacy must be sex. In fact, we're just exploring intimacy in new and different ways. It doesn't have anything to do with either sex or power."

Isabel smiled and said, "Yep, Phil, and as much as I like you, you are just the wrong gender for me. Sorry."

Allen chimed in, "Yeah, me too, roommate."

Zeke came up to their table and looked at Stella's diagram. "Ah, yes, the intimacy, sex, and power thing. You know, there are whole industries working hard to keep us confused about where we all fall on that line of intimacy and sex. The advertising and media paradigm we live in knows that sex sells. The more we connect desire, longing, yearning—and even anything physical, like touching, embracing, or caressing—with sex and the pleasure we associate with sex, the more products and commercials can be sold. So we have been thoroughly conditioned by the media and merchandisers to associate any feelings of connection and intimacy with sex.

"Although sex is a sacred and wonderfully pleasurable activity, there are many taboos, fears, commitments, and boundaries naturally associated with it. And because intimacy is so often merged with sex, many of those fears, taboos, commitments, and boundaries also get tied up with intimacy.

"We often avoid intimacy to keep ourselves from being tied up in all those confusing knots we have around sex." Zeke was silent for a moment and then walked away from the table.

Stella watched him walk away and then she turned back to the group. "This is why we have you all make that agreement with everyone else in the tribe. I bet you thought it was ridiculous to agree 'to abstain from sexual activity throughout the program with any participant you did not have a sexual relationship with prior to the start of the program.' Doesn't seem so silly now, does it? This agreement allows you to learn how to be intimate without sex making everything so messy, and without confusing intimacy with power over someone."

Emily spoke up. "God, I wish everyone had that agreement!"

The people sitting around the table laughed. Then there was a curious silence. Emily said, "I know, I know, that was a weird thing to say. It's just that last week I went on my first date since my divorce. It sucked. In this language, I was looking for some simple beginning intimacy, just to find out if I liked this guy. He was clearly looking for sex. Bottom line—he sure got to understand what 'No!' means."

Stella added, "Boy, isn't that a common tale! And that is why we introduced that guideline, so that our training didn't get contaminated with issues like the ones that came up on your messy date. We need space from all those confusing complications in order to learn how to lead powerfully.

"As leaders, we need to be very clear about the difference between sex and intimacy. When we are clear about which is which, then we can expand our ability to create genuine intimacy with others. With that unencumbered intimacy, we can be clear with, and known by, the people we are leading. We can align with and understand others much more quickly and easily."

Pointing back to her diagram, she continued, "So, that's the Intimacy-Sex line. Now let's look at the Intimacy-Power line. These are also often confused in collegial relationships, and even in friendships or connections that don't develop along sexual lines."

Allen laughed. "That's why I hate locker rooms. I mean, think of the classic 'guys in the locker room' scene. The moment a conversation heads toward a deeper connection, it usually gets deflected with one-upmanship or competition, or a stupid joke, or some other form of controlling behavior because it's getting too 'personal.' It's like guys in that setting just can't stand intimacy. There's always somebody who just has to make a joke if anyone is exposing too much tenderness."

Phil was silent. Allen was right, to a point. But it didn't always turn out like that. Some of those locker-room chats with the guys were often the closest thing he got to intimacy.

Stella said, "I don't know about guys' locker rooms. But it's not just a male thing. The same thing can be true of office colleagues. A conversation that's starting to head toward a place of deeper connection or intimacy is usually deflected into gossip or water-cooler conversation. It's just too dangerous to be open. It threatens the conventional standard that adults shouldn't have too much in the way of feelings at work. Intimacy gets sacrificed over and over again whenever there's any imagined threat to power.

"Getting back to our diagram, the art of intimacy is to be able to stay purely in the realm of intimacy and not get deflected into sex or power. When you can simply stay in intimacy, a whole new range of experiences opens up between you and another person. You all got a taste of that today, forty feet up a redwood tree. And it was more just between the two of you. Somehow you became more intimate with the whole world while you were up there.

"We often assume that intimacy is something we can create only with another person. Actually, intimacy starts inside you. It's the way you focus your own attention, allowing yourself to be vulnerable, open, receptive, and heartfelt. I can have an intimate relationship or connection with a squirrel, a forest, the universe, or even myself. I can take that focus or connection into the depths of experience with anything or everything.

"Of course, that isn't the whole picture. Intimacy doesn't have to be just a private experience. Intimacy is not just one-on-one; it can be one-on-many. When I am being held by a leader who is creating intimacy, I can be in a room of thousands of people and still feel a deep connection with, or a sense of being seen and known by, that leader. I can feel personally held even though he or she is addressing me and the mass of others around me. I feel seen into."

Phil kind of got it. He saw that he could care deeply about any number of people, including Isabel and Emily, without jeopardizing his marriage. Then he thought about having an intimate conversation with Sykes, his renegade manager. He shook his head. That was too high a bar to aim for just yet.

On the last full day of the retreat, the sound of the door closing wrenched Phil from a deep sleep. Allen must be up and leaving on a quest for his morning coffee, so Phil knew he had at least half an hour of solitude. He rolled over, pulled the covers over his head, and thought about the past week.

It looked like he was going to get that dinner after all. Zeke still hadn't won the bet. Phil had experienced a lot of cool things, but this retreat hadn't given him the answer he needed to fix his problems at work or at home. He was going to ask for that refund. Nothing he had encountered so far was going to help one whit in his relationship with Sykes, nor was it going to "transform his relationship" with Melissa. He might be able to lead standing up on a wire high in the trees, but so what? Back down here on Earth, he was still stuck.

Stella began the morning session. "Remember our circular map of the Co-Active Leadership Model? Well, up until today in this retreat, our explorations in the Leadership Model have focused primarily on all the different stages along the outside ring of the model: things like opening your awareness to the Level Three—the space and energy of the group you are leading. Then you learned to stay in that awareness until you feel an urge to act. You're starting to act on that urge in a way that marries your Level One Awareness of your desire to impact the situation with your Level Three Awareness of what's going on around you. In that action, you're allowing yourself full permission to act powerfully while taking full responsibility for how that action impacts the group or situation. And then you're taking full responsibility for cleaning up any messes that you may have created in the process of acting powerfully. You always stay fully present with the impact of your action and its consequences.

"This is what we have been talking about in these last two retreats. Now it's once again time to look into the center of this model, at the Leader's Stake."

"There are a lot of ways to lead," said Zeke. "You can demand compliance. You can manipulate. You can convince. You can impress. You can threaten. You can inspire. You can pull rank. But all of these ways of leading are based on your trying your best to get your own way, regardless of what others might want or need.

"Co-Active Leadership is powerful because everyone is aligned around a common Stake. It's a Stake that is passionately held by the leader, and it's compelling enough to ensure everyone else's participation. They want to play, too. Which naturally brings us to the question 'How does a leader get alignment and agreement around his or her Stake?'"

Zeke stood up, walked over to the easel, and flipped over to a new page. On it was written:

Agreement ⟶ Understanding ⟶ Acceptance

"Most of us converse or connect with each other through this filter most of the time. Before we look for someone to align with us, we make sure we establish our own point of view and commit to it.

Then we enter the conversation and look for the other person to agree with our point of view.

"Unfortunately, the more we look for agreement, the more we have to explain and defend our point of view. As a result of all that clarifying and justification, we get to be more and more rigidly set in that point of view. Now it must be true! We are less and less open to deeply listening to the other person. We often discover that we can't get past this place of trying to convince the other person that we are right and they are wrong. This lack of agreement can easily turn into conflict and argument. That's when all sorts of reactive and defensive behaviors start to show up."

Phil thought Zeke must have been sitting in on those meetings he had with Bill Sykes, and on his dinner conversations at home.

Stella continued, "Sometimes we can sort through it all and reach a place on this diagram that I call 'Understanding.' This is the place where we can say, 'I understand your point of view, and you understand my point of view.' This can lead to a fairly civil place where either we respect our different points of view or we reach some sort of compromise that we can both agree on and live with. 'Agreement' is the most important value in this string; it's the necessary precursor for moving on. So at this stage, either we respectfully disagree or we compromise our points of view to reach a place where we can agree.

"In this way of relating to each other, the final place we reach, if we're really lucky, is 'Acceptance.' Sometimes what emerges from that place of understanding is an acceptance of the other person, of who they are and what they stand for. In that acceptance, there is still room for our differences. However, let's face it, most of us never reach this point. Most of the time, we have been pulled off this path by all of the unwilling compromises and resentful sacrifices we had to go through, just to get from Agreement to Understanding. We rarely make it all the way to Acceptance and usually settle for a reluctant compliance."

Phil thought to himself, *In my case*, rarely *is an exaggeration; more like* never.

Then Zeke turned to the next page on the easel.

Acceptance → Alignment → Understanding → Agreement

"In the Co-Active Leadership Model, we want to turn this process inside out. Instead of looking for Agreement in order to get to Acceptance, we start with Acceptance and end up at Agreement. In this conversation, we each begin from an Acceptance of the other and we set an intention to co-create Alignment, Understanding, and Agreement arising from that Acceptance.

"The first stage of acceptance is an inside job. We have to face the futility of trying to prove to the other person that we are wiser, better, and more knowledgeable than they are. We must take as an act of faith the belief that the other person is naturally creative, resourceful, and whole, and that he or she is sincerely looking for a solution, not engaged in an endless battle for control. When we adopt this perspective, sometimes it has the almost magical effect of shifting the energy between you and the person you have a conflict with. When one side won't fight any more, suddenly the war is over.

"How do we start out from a place of Alignment? Well, we have to find our common ground. We need to align around something bigger than just our own separate points of view on an issue. Here is where a Stake we both desire is so important. Where is that passionate point of intersection of mission, ideals, and shared goals where we can meet as equals, each of us passionately in agreement with the Stake? We align around a Stake that embodies who we all are and what it is that we're up to. We may have to poke and prod, expand and open up our awareness as we look for this place of alignment.

Stella got up and walked over to the chart. "Once we find that shared place of alignment, then we can create from the disagreements and differences, instead of allowing them to dominate. As we push and pull and agree and disagree, we begin to truly understand each other. With this understanding, we can begin to completely celebrate and enjoy our differences and our disagreements as we work our way along this aligned path."

Zeke joined her on the other side of the easel. "See, Agreement now becomes the last element in the string, and the least important. In fact, disagreement is valued just as much as agreement. I don't just respect your opinions and your differences; I'm deeply curious about them. Now they're something I can create from as we continue down this path together, and you feel the same way about disagreements with me. Our egos are much more in check, and we can create stuff together that neither of us could have done by ourselves.

"Sure," Phil muttered to himself, "that sounds great in theory. But just try doing it out there in the real world!"

Stella said, "Okay, so now you are going to try it. Find a partner, find a topic you disagree on, and practice using this new process."

Emily came at Phil like a heat-seeking missile. She smiled and said, "Let's talk about weight."

"Sure," he said, with an attempt at a smile, even though he could feel the antagonism rising up inside.

Emily started off. "Okay, so we already know there is disagreement, and some judgment, probably going both ways about this. Let's see where we can align around it."

Phil said, "Yeah, sure, I'm willing!" He added to himself, *Maybe*.

"So, I feel people come in all sizes and should not be judged for their size."

Phil immediately found himself disagreeing with this idea. But before he launched his counter-attack, he remembered a tool from the theater improv they had done earlier in the retreat. In this planning/brainstorming exercise, one person listened to whatever his partner said, replied with, "What I like about your idea is . . . ," and then added something positive and constructive. This had gone on for five minutes, each person starting his or her response with, "What I like about your idea is . . ." That way, no ideas were judged as wrong, and each one built upon the previous one. He decided to try it.

"What I like about your idea is that it doesn't judge anybody, and I think that carrying around too much weight can be unhealthy."

Emily laughed and then picked up on his cue. "What I like about your idea is that it's concerned about people's health, and I think that, while obesity is unhealthy, there is still a wide range of healthy weights people can have."

Stella was walking by and overheard the last part of this dialogue. She interrupted, "Emily, that was really a 'Yes . . . But' statement, not a 'Yes . . . And' statement. A 'Yes . . . But' statement basically says, 'Sure, I will pretend to agree, but here is why you are wrong.' A 'Yes . . . And' statement truly builds on what the other person said."

Emily took another crack at it. "Okay, Phil. What I like about your idea is that you are concerned about what is healthy, and I actually share your concerns about obesity, and I am curious about where the demarcation lies for you between largeness and obesity. I wonder how you make the distinction between being unhealthily overweight and just having a large, healthy frame."

Phil sighed. This was hard! "What I like about your idea is that it distinguishes between unhealthy overweight and healthy bigness, and I imagine that a woman finds it harder to be attractive when she is big, even if she is healthy. I really can't speak for women, but I know that I'm more attracted to slimmer women myself."

Emily was silent for a while, but her eyes were bright. He worried that she was going to blast him. Then she spoke.

"What I like about your idea is that it accurately reflects a lot of opinions of the popular culture. And I think there are women, and men, for that matter, who just don't want to fit into that rigid stereotype. God knows, I don't want to be put into a box, and I bet you don't either. Men and women can love themselves regardless of their size, and can love others regardless of the common media-inspired obsession with slenderness.

"Now, that's not to say that there aren't health risks associated with obesity, just as there are with anorexia. But a healthy body can come in many shapes."

Stella left. They were doing fine.

Phil was silent for a long time. What Emily had said hit him very hard. For him, the issue was a lot bigger than someone's being overweight. It was about those boxes everyone else constructed around him. He saw how Bill Sykes, the current bane of his existence, had Phil shoved into a box labeled **The new young guy who stole my promotion**. His wife had him jammed into her box of **All he really cares about is his work**. Suddenly, he knew what it felt like to be criticized for things he didn't deserve to be judged on. And here he had been doing the same thing to Emily. He looked over at her. She actually *was* attractive—both plump and attractive.

He said, "I think there's a place where we can find some alignment. I'm facing the same kind of harsh criticism at my job that you probably get sometimes for your weight. Hell, I'm facing the same kind of thing with my wife, too. I can see I might be doing some unfair prejudgment with you. I'm sorry."

Emily smiled tentatively. "Yes, it's true. I get judged a lot by men and by women. So I can see that you might get a little taste of what it feels like when you think about how that manager you keep talking about treats you."

"Yes," Phil said. "I never seem to be good enough."

Emily's smile widened. "And I never seem to be thin enough."

They both laughed. Then Phil said, "So we can align around the experience that being judged really sucks."

Emily added, "And hurts!" Then there was a pause where they just looked at each other, each one seeing the pain in the other's eyes.

"So we may not ever agree on the ideal weight someone should be, but we can agree that, assuming they are not self-destructively obese, judging them isn't helpful."

"How about we agree that other people's weight is actually none of our business?"

Phil held out his hand to shake. "Deal."

Emily took his hand, and instead of shaking it, she just held it. They sat there for a while, holding each other's hands. "So, tell me about your wife," she said.

On the last day of the retreat, at the closing ceremony, Phil was feeling very complete. Then Allen stood up to speak and surprised them all.

"I wrote a poem about that first leaning-into-each-other event on the ropes course. It isn't really about me, because Emily and I fell right off. I wrote it after watching Phil and Olivia and how they so supported each other. So this poem is dedicated to them. I call it 'Lean In.' Here it goes."

Lean In
Today you no longer need
to wake, sigh, and hoist the world
back up on your weary shoulders.
Lean in.

Today you no longer need
to walk the twisted pathway that you call your life,
legs moving mechanically, heart frozen,
resigned to your loneliness.
Lean in.

Remember,
you were there before the beginning of time,

when that vast ball of yet-to-be
got so sick of being alone
that it burst into ten trillion lovers.

Remember,
you were there at the birth of creation,
when all things were securely wrapped round
with caring cords of gravity;
eternally connecting everything with everything else.

Remember,
You were there. Yet you forgot.
We were there, yet we forgot.
We made up the tragic tale that we were all alone.

On chubby legs and half-grown bones
we stumbled forth into a dangerous world,
pretending that we needed no support,
trying not to cry each time we fell.

We forgot—until today.
Now it all comes back.
We were always home, in the house we never knew.
To walk right through that door, all we must do
is fiercely lean in, holding nothing back.
In doing that, we might call forth
a world full of eager loving arms.

Yes, eventually we fall,
too weak to hold ourselves erect much longer,
too scared to give the other any more,
too trusting of a partner
who no longer can return our gift.

We fall, but someone holds us on belay.

Oh, we may get a bruise or two,
our heart gets knocked around a bit,
our plans and dreams end up scattered on the ground.
But we climb back up again, because we know we must,
because something unknowable is calling us to climb.

And now we feel the other leaning into us.
And now we feel everything leaning into us.
We no longer need to fear the fall.
Everywhere is home, and gravity reveals its warm true
nature.
It's love. All is love. Just love.

Standing by the bus, waiting to leave the retreat center for the airport, Phil watched as other tribemates swarmed around Zeke and Stella to say good-bye. When the crowd thinned enough around Zeke, Phil walked over and handed him a check.

"Dirty trick, waiting for the last day to hook me. But you win. I think I have something I can use. Wish me luck, because if this blows up and I get fired or divorced, I'll hunt you down."

Zeke laughed. "You know, somehow I don't think I have anything to fear. It's been quite a retreat, hasn't it? I am glad you got something from this. Be sure to write me and tell me what happens with you and Mr. Sykes."

"Deal."

Phil shook Zeke's hand, smiled, and got on the bus. This next week was going to be very interesting.

Isabel's silver Lexus was the last of the Unicorn Tribe's cars to pull out of the retreat parking lot. Zeke and Stella watched as her car disappeared around the bend.

Zeke put his arm around Stella's shoulders, and she put her arm around his waist. They just stood there quietly.

Finally Zeke said, "I hate it when my personal life interferes with my leading. Imperfection tastes lousy. I'm pretty pissed that Jason had such rotten timing. But I can't really blame it all on him. You know, I really love doing this work. I'm sorry that I stumbled there for a couple of days."

Stella looked up at him. "You didn't stumble. Your heart broke a little, but it just made you more open to the group. And you leaned on me. That meant so much. Thank you for trusting me. You want me to kick Jason's butt?"

Zeke smiled. "I'll call if I need you."

Stella said, "Good idea, Zeke. Call me if you need to. I'm on the res until our next retreat."

He roughed up her hair. "I might, Raven. I just might."

Key Leadership Concepts in Retreat Two

Relationship is at the center of everything we do as leaders.

Intimacy comes when we let go of our expectations and judgments about the other person and just get curious about who is over there in the other chair. You need both faces of intimacy: the capacity to really see the other person and the capacity to reveal your truest self. Intimacy is not just one-on-one; it can be one-on-many. I can be in a room of thousands of people and feel a deep connection with, or a sense of being seen and known by, the leader.

Assumptions: When I have an assumption about you, I am no longer able to see you or know you. Instead, I am seeing my opinions about you. I can see or know you only through the veil of that assumption. One of the most powerful agreements we can make as leaders is to strive to clear out the assumptions we make about each other that get in the way of clear communication and intimacy.

Clearing Assumptions: The person clearing the assumption must be committed to clearing the assumption. The person clearing the assumption needs to keep looking underneath the surface of the assumption to get to the underlying beliefs or assumptions that he or she is holding. The witness's job is *not* to coach or advise the person with the assumption, but just to listen deeply and "feel" into whether or not the energy of the person doing the clearing is feeling clearer.

Co-leadership: When two leaders are leading a room at the same time, both are equally responsible for what happens. Both of them need to be entirely unique and powerful in their own right. In order for co-leadership to work, the belief that each leader brings 50 percent to the task of leading a room or a team needs to be tossed out. There is plenty of room for both leaders to bring 100 percent of themselves 100 percent of the time. Your goal as a co-leader is not to fit smoothly into the shape of your co-leader. It is not to avoid stepping on his or her toes. It is not to always blend together perfectly, never making waves. Your goal as a co-leader is to play full out, to love that your co-leader is also playing full out, and for both of you to serve your shared Stake.

Creating with other: We are used to creating *with* other people. Those relationships look like this: Side by side with another, I go through life. I brainstorm, collaborate, and create this project with this or that other person. In an ideal side-by-side 'with' relationship, I bring 50 percent and you bring 50 percent. More often, one person brings some percentage greater or less than that 50 percent, and the other person balances it out.

Creating from other is much more powerful. In this kind of relationship, I turn to face you. Then I focus my full attention on both seeing and knowing you and on opening myself up to be seen and known by you. When I include you and see into you, I am in a position to go beyond merely creating "with" you. We are now able to be fully present with each other, and each of us contributes 100 percent of our self to whatever endeavor we are engaged in together.

Sourcing: Once you are able to create a strong Level Two connection with someone, you can then consciously be a source of their success. You can focus your attention on what it is that they are doing, the risks they are taking, and the moves they are making. Then you can be the source of their finding the extra inch or the extra ounce of energy to cross that last gap.

Intimacy-Sex-Power:

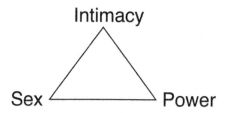

So much acute suffering in relationships, at work and in our lives, comes from ignorance about the principles that are expressed in the Intimacy-Sex-Power triangle. We take sex for intimacy, seek power through sex, think power is really intimacy, and every other combination imaginable. What often happens as we begin to let ourselves feel the attraction of that intimacy is that we get confused, thinking this connection we feel is about sexual attraction. We fear that the eventual end of this intimacy must be sex. In fact, it's just the energy of exploring intimacy in new and different ways and doesn't have anything to do with either sex or power. As leaders, we need to know clearly what sex is and what intimacy is. When we are clear about what is what, then we can safely expand our ability to create genuine intimacy with others.

Intimacy happens inside you. We assume that intimacy is something we create with another person. Actually, intimacy happens inside. It is the way you focus your own attention, allowing yourself to be vulnerable, open, receptive, and heartfelt. You can have an intimate relationship or connection with a squirrel, a forest, the universe, or even yourself. You can take that focus or connection into the depths of experience with anything or everything.

The Old Model of Achieving Alignment and Managing Conflict:

Agreement ⟶ Understanding ⟶ Acceptance

1. Start the conversation by looking for agreement with our point of view.

2. Reach a place of "I understand your point of view, and you understand my point of view."

3. We rarely reach Acceptance and usually settle for reluctant compliance.

The New Model:

Acceptance → Alignment → Understanding → Agreement

1. Starting with an acceptance of the other and ourselves, we set an intention to create together an alignment and agreement arising from that acceptance.

2. We align on something that would include our possible differences.

3. In this understanding, we can begin to completely celebrate and enjoy our differences and our disagreement as we work our way down this aligned path. Agreement now becomes the last element in the string and the least important. In fact, disagreement is valued just as much as agreement. We don't just respect each other's opinions and differences; we are deeply curious about them. They are something we can now create from as we continue down this path together.

A Six-Step Conflict Management Tool: Instead of striving to reduce conflict, this tool welcomes conflict as a creative process for discovering unimagined solutions.

TRANSFORMING CONFLICT

Step 1 NOTICE YOUR REACTION.
Either notice your need to be right, and to win at all costs, or notice your need to capitulate and betray your own point of view.

Step 2 PAUSE.
Take a breath before you speak. Or maybe two.

Step 3 ALIGN.
Seek alignment about something *beyond* or something *more important* than the issue in conflict, something that supersedes the topic you disagree about.

Step 4 UNDERSTAND.
Once alignment is reached, seek to understand the other person's point of view from that place of alignment.

Step 5 DISAGREE/AGREE.
From this new place of understanding and alignment, go ahead and have the disagreement, for the sake of coming up with a creative solution.

Step 6 CHOOSE.
Choose a creative solution to the conflict that you both can live with.

Chapter Five

Journey into Conflict

The encouraging thing is that every time you meet a situation, though you may think at the time it is an impossibility and you go through the tortures of the damned, once you have met it and lived through it you find that forever after you are freer than you ever were before. If you can live through that you can live through anything. You gain strength, courage, and confidence by every experience in which you stop to look fear in the face. You are able to say to yourself, 'I lived through this horror. I can take the next thing that comes along.' The danger lies in refusing to face the fear, in not daring to come to grips with it. If you fail anywhere along the line, it will take away your confidence. You must make yourself succeed every time. You must do the thing you think you cannot do.

Eleanor Roosevelt

Phil **was** sitting at his dining room table, looking into Melissa's angry brown eyes. "Look, honey, I know it has been pretty crummy between us this past few months."

"You can say that again," she snapped. "Ever since your job got changed, it's like you aren't around anymore, or if you are here, you're still thinking about work. It's all you ever talk about anymore! That and your precious Unicorns!"

Phil could feel his Destructive-Self, Level-One demon start to rise up and yell at her, *I'm doing it all for you, and you don't appreciate me!* But he stopped that demon dead in its tracks. That demon had done enough damage to their relationship.

He took a deep breath and looked around the room. The Sarah Waldron oil painting they had bought on their honeymoon caught his eye. It was a beautiful, impressionist painting of koi swimming through deep blue water. Yes, he needed some of that calm gracefulness right now.

His Stake for this conversation was clear: "Our love can overcome all our negative junk." And he knew that there was still a part of both of them that accepted without question that this marriage was worth saving. So he started to seek alignment, instead of trying to get her to agree with his position that he was making all these heroic sacrifices for her.

He said, "Yeah, you're right. I have been pretty obsessed lately. But while I was on retreat last week, I got clear that our marriage is a lot more important to me than my relationship with some stupid Southern California manager. I really don't want to screw us up, and I think I have been doing that lately. You and me, that's the most important thing, right?"

Melissa gave him a hard look. "Well, you haven't been acting like that was the most important thing."

Phil had to keep reminding himself that she hadn't gone to the retreat, and that she was still lodged firmly in a "fight to win" model. So he decided to meet her where she obviously needed to be met. He took a deep breath and gave it another shot.

"I think we can both agree that things have been pretty difficult between us lately. And that my actions have been a lot more focused on me-me-me than on us. I remember that night last year on the cruise ship. We were sitting on the promenade deck in the moonlight, and you said to me, 'Let's have a baby.' We were so close in that moment. And I know we both still really want this baby!"

She smiled at him, the first completely warm, open smile that he could remember in months. She said, "Yeah, we do."

Phil went on, "I get how new and scary this must be for you. Neither of us has ever done anything like this before. And I also get how my working extra hours these past few weeks must have felt like I am deserting you when you need me the most."

She said, "Yes, it has. And I know work has been really rough. But I do need more of you."

Phil admitted, "I get scared they're going to fire me or demote me if I mishandle this whole Bill Sykes mess. That's the last thing we need right now!"

Then she took his hands. "I don't want you to get fired. But if you do, well, then we'll just cope with it. I love you and I miss you. Don't get lost at work. Come home to me."

"I love you too, Melissa. More than anything. Just know that when I am stuck at work, it's because I have to be there and I will do what I can to get back home where I really want to be, by your side. Sometimes I can't, and it's okay to get pissed at me. Just know that you and our family are my number-one priority."

It wasn't all fixed. But as they lay in each other's arms that night, Phil knew they were going to get through this.

It **was** two days before they were due to present their workshop on gratitude to a small group at Isabel's Center. Isabel and Phil were meeting over lattés at a local coffee shop to do some more planning.

Phil wasn't into it. "So, what the hell are we going to do for this damn project? I'm not feeling very grateful right now, and a workshop on Gratitude feels pretty boring."

Isabel smiled. "Stop whining, Phil. Let's figure out how to do this together."

Boy, she was direct. Phil smiled back. Direct and right on: he *had* been playing "poor me." He felt how much he trusted her forthright honesty. He wished he had her in his office. Suddenly a light went on, and he started laughing.

"Hey, Isabel, what do you think about tossing out the whole gratitude thing? Let's start from scratch. How about doing a workshop on conflict management at my company, with my team? We'll invite my nemesis, Bill Sykes, aka the Marquis de Sade, and you can fix him!"

Isabel smiled a smile that had a hint of evil delight in it. Then she said, "Oh, yes, sign me up. It sounds like both of you definitely need some fixing. That's pure genius! And I'd love to work on that model. The whole Acceptance-Understanding-Alignment thing is too academic. I'd love to see if we can translate it into simple, direct steps. Here's how we can start out . . ."

Showtime! **Phil** looked down the conference-room table at the group waiting quietly for them to begin. Isabel was by his side, looking very corporate executive in her navy blazer and skirt. He couldn't have had better backup. Thank heavens he hadn't partnered with Allen, who probably would have come in blue jeans. He had time to look over his group while Isabel was doing her introduction.

She said, "Conflict costs businesses untold millions of dollars and exacts an even greater toll in negative morale, lost jobs, and unhappy lives. There are plenty of workshops out there that teach you how to manage, negotiate, or resolve conflict. Basically, they all focus on giving you the tools for finding the shortest route to defusing and eliminating conflict.

"Our approach today will be very different. Instead of avoiding or shutting down conflict, we're training you to engage with it, to use it as a creative opportunity to develop new solutions to existing problems and situations. Sounds ambitious, we know, but through using these practices, we believe turf wars can be turned into productive brainstorming sessions. Does that sound worth your afternoon?"

Phil saw mild interest in the faces of the others sitting around the table. There were nine participants. Five of them worked in this building and reported directly to Phil. There were three people from other departments who had heard about this particular workshop through the grapevine. And, of course, there was Phil's favorite manager, Bill Sykes.

Phil led them through an icebreaker exercise where they all introduced themselves and shared a little-known fact about their lives (and Phil learned that his nemesis collected model railroad cars). Then Isabel sat down and Phil turned over a page of the flip chart to reveal their six-step list for transforming conflict.

TRANSFORMING CONFLICT

Step 1 NOTICE YOUR REACTION.
Either notice your need to be right, and to win at all costs, or notice your need to capitulate and betray your own point of view.

Step 2 PAUSE.
Take a breath before you speak. Or maybe two.

Step 3 ALIGN.
Seek alignment about something *beyond* or something *more important* than the issue in conflict, something that supersedes the topic you disagree about.

Step 4 UNDERSTAND.
Once alignment is reached, seek to understand the other person's point of view from that place of alignment.

Step 5 DISAGREE/AGREE.
From this new place of understanding and alignment, go ahead and have the disagreement, for the sake of coming up with a creative solution.

Step 6 CHOOSE.
Choose a creative solution to the conflict that you both can live with.

Phil launched into the meat of the workshop. "Okay, the first thing we usually want to do in any disagreement is to convince the other person that our position is the correct one. That works in only two situations: one is when the other person is already in agreement, and the other, more common one is when they are just wanting to kiss up to us.

"The rest of the time, our efforts to make them agree with us only seem to make things worse. The other person keeps stubbornly repeating their obviously inferior position, and we keep on trying to reframe our superior position so that even a moron could understand it."

At this line, laughter broke out around the table.

"So, instead of that rather unsuccessful approach, we want you to try something else. The first step is to recognize that you are in one of those messy impasse situations where it seems that someone is going to win and someone is going to lose and resent losing. We call this a 'win-lose' scenario, and it always leaves at least one of the participants dissatisfied and wanting to get even the next time."

Isabel stood up. "Recognizing that you are hip-deep in yet another swamp is the beginning of taking Step One: Notice your Reaction. Go ahead and feel the irritation that arises in you when the other person doesn't just fall all over himself, loving your idea. But this time, rather than acting on your frustration, you don't launch yet another offensive in order to extract an agreement from the other person. You don't dive in and engage in all those unsatisfying and ultimately unsuccessful activities, like blaming and defending. You don't continue dishing up more explanations, in ever-simpler terms, and you definitely don't collapse and give up. Instead, you notice that you are feeling frustrated. Then you just take a deep breath, maybe two, which gives you time to remember that you have some other tools in your toolbox besides weapons. And guess what? You just took Step Two: Pause."

Phil could read the doubt on Bill Sykes's face, but he let Isabel go on.

"This next step—Step Three: Align—is the tricky part. You're going to do something very different from fighting to win or giving up in defeat. You're going to have to leave behind the 'I must win!' position and step into the place of 'How can we create from this mess?'

"And before you can do that, you must find out what the two of you share in common, what connects the two of you. What is your common territory? From that shared base, you can look at the problem with new eyes. Now you can welcome contrasting views of possible solutions. Often a dynamic, unexpected new solution emerges from this intense dialogue."

Now Phil could see another look slide across Sykes's face; he interpreted it as boredom, and he decided to jump in. "We're going to show you some helpful questions that we created. In and of themselves, they will not do the job, but they can begin to reorient the conversation away from just butting horns.

"Remember, the purpose of this work is not to 'cool the mark.' Let me tell you what I mean by that phrase. It comes from the circus. In carnivals, most of the money is made at the skill stands, where people pitch pennies, shoot guns, or throw balls to win a prize. These games, of course, are rigged so that it's darn hard to walk away with a stuffed panda. Sometimes customers (called 'marks' by the folks who work those carnival booths) begin to get a little teed off.

"At that point, a signal goes out and a member of the carnival staff, disguised as a fellow tourist, comes over and starts losing big-time, right next to the person getting angry. But the imposter laughs and appears to be having a great time losing a lot of money. This placates most customers, who walk off thinking, *Well, at least I didn't lose as much as that jerk did*. This is what is referred to as 'cooling the mark.'"

Isabel picked it up: "We feel too much of what passes as conflict management is more about 'cooling the mark' than it is about creating real change. We don't just want peace at any price. That is why we support disagreeing views and feel that a good, healthy disagreement can lead to real innovation.

"So your goal in using these questions isn't to get the other person to calm down. It's to see where you share common ground, and then, from that shared space, to surface the differences and explore them, knowing that both of you are on the same team. That is how you get away from the win-lose mentality."

She turned to the next flip-chart page. "As you go through this process, ask each one of these questions, and then also answer them yourself, out loud, right before or after the other person does. Remember, always listen to the concerns of the other person, and ask about those concerns in relationship to your problem. Know that this conflict can lead to innovation. Stay grounded in the alignment! The two of you are always looking for common ground. That way, both of you can learn something."

CONFLICT MANAGEMENT QUESTIONS

1 **UNDERSTANDING Question**
   Why is this problem important for us to focus on?

2 **AGREE/DISAGREE Question**
   What do you see as the area of disagreement between us?

3 **ALIGNMENT Question**
   What can we align on that is outside the problem itself?

4 **UNDERSTANDING Questions**
   What is behind *your* point of view about the problem?
   What resources can we bring to the solution?
   What other possible solutions are there to this problem?

5 **AGREE/DISAGREE Question**
   What solution can we create from our disagreement about the problem that we both can live with and grow with?

6 **CHOOSE Question**
   How do you see the two of us working together on this?

Phil continued. "So, the first question you should ask is the Understanding question: 'Why is this problem important for us to focus on?' Then you follow that up with the Agree/Disagree question: 'What do you see as the area of disagreement between us?' Now, be careful. This isn't an invitation to jump back into the fire. Let the other person go first, and encourage him or her to bottom-line what his or her perspective on the situation is. Then you do the same, not commenting on or judging what you see or what they saw, just putting out how you understand the problem. Keep this part short and crisp; just make it an overview of the situation from each of your perspectives."

Isabel stepped in. "The next question to ask is the Alignment question: 'What can we align on that is outside the problem itself?' This is the step that takes both of you out of the swamp. Instead of looking at the conflict and trying to find some territory inside the disagreement where you can meet, you step outside the territory of the conflict. You both look for a place where you can meet in alignment."

Phil said, "We're not talking of alignment about irrelevant issues, like both rooting for the Giants. But look for an alignment above the place where you disagree, on a higher level, as it were. For instance, you both may completely disagree about merging the advertising and the marketing departments into one. But you can align around how getting the word out there to the public about the quality of your product is crucial to the success of your enterprise."

Isabel turned the chart back to their six-step list.

"Step Four is 'Understanding.' In this step, each of you is looking to really understand what's behind the position that your adversary has been taking. What beliefs, values, or perceptions about the situation are they holding that led them to taking their position? Keep asking for clarification, not with a desire to prove them wrong, but just with a sincere curiosity about why they think the way they do about this situation.

"Sometimes it helps if you just repeat back to them what they said, so that they know you heard them. With Phil's example, it might look something like, 'So, if I understand you correctly, the way you see it is that the people in marketing already feel like second-class citizens in comparison with those in advertising, and this would just make that morale problem worse.' We call this process of repeating back what you just heard 'mirroring.'"

Phil loved how she just picked up his example and danced with it. Isabel went on, "When it's your turn, keep your statement about what is behind your position crisp and short. There is no need to beat him or her over the head with your opinion—just cut to the essence of your position."

Phil added, "So the goal of all this isn't to convince anyone that yours is the best position. You are fully understanding the other's position, and speaking clearly about your position in order to enter cleanly into the heart of the conflict."

Pointing to Step Five: Disagree/Agree, he said, "The next phase of this process may get a little hot. It's okay to disagree when both of you are aligned about where you are heading. With the ends clearly shared, then the whole discussion becomes how to best achieve those ends. Out of disagreement comes the greatest creativity. Instead of being in opposing camps, you are on the same team, ultimately wanting the same thing, with differing ideas about how to get it. That kind of interaction can be fiery and vocal, but it's fun, because it no longer involves anyone losing the war. The rest of the questions are fuel for that creative process."

Isabel sat back down at the conference table as she spoke. "All these are really great ideas. And they lead to Step Six: 'Choose a creative solution to the conflict that you both can live with.' But I bet a few of you are saying, 'Yeah, sure, great idea. But how the heck do I do it?'" There were a few nods.

She went on, "So now we're going to split everyone into pairs to practice this part of the skill. Because there are an uneven number of participants, Phil will participate, and I will go around and coach each pair about how to go through this process."

Phil saw a perfect opportunity to begin some work with the dreaded Bill Sykes. Isabel gave him a subtle pat of encouragement on his back as he walked over to sit next to Sykes. Bill looked up at him and smiled.

"Well, Phil, do we have anything we disagree about?"

Phil smiled back and said, "Oh, I think we can find something to practice this with."

Within two minutes, both of them were sitting back, arms crossed, faces flushed and frowning. Phil was saying, "Bill, I'm all for employee loyalty, but you don't understand the pressure I'm under from New York. We have to make some painful cuts, and a good place to start is our call center. Outsourcing that—"

Sykes cut him off, "You're just robbing Peter to pay Paul. Look, the savings of a few cents per call can never offset the impact on my workforce as department after department gets hacked away. You're going to lose the best . . ."

Hearing the raised voices, Isabel came over, bringing a cup of coffee for each contender. She set one cup in front of Sykes, who stopped his tirade to thank her. Then she put her hand on Phil's shoulder and said to him, "Call me 'honey,' and you know where this cup is going to end up." Phil laughed.

Then she looked down at both of them. "Bill! Phil! Both of you, just stop for a second. You know each other's position on this. This is a perfect subject for trying out this new approach. Are you game to try it?"

Sykes didn't stop frowning, but he took a sip of his coffee and gave a little nod.

Phil started in, "Okay. So let's find some alignment. The first question is 'Why is this problem important for us to focus on?'"

Isabel interrupted and said, "Hold your horses here, Phil. I don't think you took the first step, which is to notice your reaction. First, each of you take a moment to notice yourselves in reaction. Step above all your feelings, and activate that neutral observer. Recognize what it feels like in your body to be convinced that you are *right* and that the other person must be *wrong*. Notice that you feel like you are in some familiar, old, and hopeless pattern that seems to have no way out."

At first, Phil got angry at Isabel for interrupting him. Then he realized that he was in a sort of fake neutrality, just going through the motions of doing the exercise while all the time being sure that he was right. He felt how tight his belly was in that moment.

"Good," she continued. "Now pause and take a breath. I am betting that you two are sick of fighting over this issue and all the other little issues that have preceded it." They both nodded.

"Then find an intention to discover a creative solution to this problem that is outside the box of all the solutions you have already chewed over—a solution that lives out beyond the territory that you are already familiar with." Isabel could feel the shift in the atmosphere between the two men, a slight easing of tension. Then she said, "Excellent. Now, Phil, start with your questions."

With a quick glance of admiration at Isabel, Phil stopped looking over at the chart and asked his question in another way: "What are the key drivers to our business that we need to achieve? That might give us something that we can align on."

As he counted off on his fingers, Sykes said, "Well, of course there's profitability, ROI, market share, customer satisfaction, and employee satisfaction."

Phil agreed. "Yep, those are the metrics that we must pay attention to. Those are the numbers that we watch and base all our decisions on."

Sykes said, "I think the ones that are most critical to the issue of call centers are the last two. Would you agree?"

Phil felt the desire to start another fight. Then he realized that there was a lot of truth in what Sykes had just said. He answered, "Well, I think that all of them come into the mix with any big decision we are going to make. Certainly, we don't want to turn our back on profitability. But the uproar we had in our call center last month has a lot to do with this mess we are in right now, so I agree that the conflict we are having needs to take into account employee satisfaction."

Isabel could see that they were beginning on the road to alignment and moved off to another pair to check on how they were doing moving through the questions.

A little while later, she came back to check in on them. Sykes was saying, "Okay. So, if I understand what you are saying, your ass is in a sling from the East Coast about profitability."

Phil laughed. "Exactly! And if I get what you said, there will be hell to pay if a bunch of pink slips show up in people's paychecks."

Sykes smiled. "You got that right."

They were getting it. Isabel moved on.

A few minutes later, she said in a loud voice, "Okay, everyone. Stop what you are doing for a moment. Let's check in and see how this process is working. Who would like to report out how it's going?"

The first group to report had lost their focus and regressed into arguing over the circumstances. Another group was doing great. Then Sykes raised his hand and said, "I am sort of amazed that it can be this easy both to be understood and to understand someone else, and I'm really curious to see what we can create from our disagreement." Phil shrugged his shoulders, smiled at Isabel, and gave her a nod.

Isabel smiled back, then said to the group, "Well, great—most of you should be at the point that Phil and Bill are at in their conversation. You've recognized your reaction, found a place to align, created understanding, and are now ready to have a creative disagreement about the original topic, so start your engines and disagree. I'll come over and help the first group over there get back on track."

A few minutes later, Isabel heard a loud bark of a laugh, looked across the room, and saw that Sykes was actually laughing, while Phil had a goofy smile on his face. She went over to see what was going on. Sykes looked up at her and said, "Well, we went back to the disagreement about the call center going overseas. We both batted around our viewpoints, but we couldn't really defend them like we used to. So we began to come up with other ways to look at it and then disagreed about all of those, until this totally strange idea popped out of Phil's mouth. Both of us went wide-eyed over it, and we began to laugh at its sheer perfection."

"That's right," Phil chuckled, as he shook his head. "Hey, what do you know! This stuff I'm teaching really works. Bill and I are coming up with an idea for a web-based customer-service/call-center operation, a kind that has never been tried before. We're wondering if we can make it scalable and market it to other industries."

"So when can we get together and hammer this out, Phil?" Sykes said as he pulled out his iPhone. But Phil didn't get a chance to make that appointment. Just then, Saul, his executive administrator, came rushing in.

"Baby on its way, Phil. Head straight for the hospital; Melissa's mom is driving her there!"

Phil stood beside the operating table, holding his new daughter, as the nurses took care of his wife. The baby's small head rested comfortably in the palm of his hand. She opened her indigo-blue eyes, and Phil felt that he could look right through them into the heart of creation. He felt relays clicking deep in his soul, and he knew he was linked to this new being until his last breath.

She smiled, almost as though she agreed, and he began to cry. He told her, "You know, little one, Zeke was only half right. Sure, you create from other. But you are created from other, too. You sure are creating me right now, aren't you?"

His daughter gurgled.

Chapter Six

Creating from Nothing

A leader is a dealer in hope.

Napoleon Bonaparte

Isabel stood outside the door to her mother's room in the skilled-nursing facility, unable to push it open. She was so ashamed at how vulnerable she felt. An unexpected memory came to her: being up on the high ropes, climbing this oversize ladder, feeling a bit annoyed, and holding on to Emily. Emily was out of shape, a bit nervous, and her weight was making this event very difficult for her. Isabel was in much better shape, so she was taking the lead. They were not doing very well, and she blamed Emily for that.

Suddenly, Emily shouted at her, "Isabel, stop being in control. You are screwing us up. You're not leading; you're dragging me. Look down here at me, and let yourself need a partner!"

Letting herself need a partner was an underdeveloped muscle for Isabel. The two of them had fallen off the ladder soon after that outburst, and Isabel knew it was because she had no idea how to use Emily's resources and strengths. She didn't know how to lean on someone else, to let herself actually need another person. Her life partner, Violet, continually complained that Isabel always felt like she had to step in and do it all.

Well, she needed someone right now. The doctor had left her at the door, and now she could not bring herself to open it. Luckily, there was no one in the hall to see her. She just stood there, frozen, for a long time.

As she stood there, unable to act, her sister, Josephina, came walking around the corner.

"Isabel, you came. These visits are just getting worse and worse. I guess you knew, right? I am so glad you're here. Thank God. I am so glad you're here. I really need the company. Come on, let's go in together." As Josephina spoke, something quite remarkable happened to Isabel. It was as though the hall suddenly became lighter. The air was not as sour smelling, and Isabel found she could take a deeper breath.

Josephina pushed open the door. Their mother was in a wheelchair, looking out the window. She turned and smiled and said, "Isabel!" Isabel relaxed even more. Then her mother said, *"Llévame a casa ahora. ¿Por qué estoy aquí? No me gusta esa lugar. Llévame a casa. ¡Por favor!"*

Josephina took her mother's hand. Isabel sighed and said, "We can't take you home, Mama. You are in a nice place where people can take care of you. It's going to be okay."

What was she going to do about her mother? The visits were always a burdensome duty. Her mother always made her feel guilty when she begged to be taken home, which happened just about every visit now. But Isabel had no words to comfort her. And if she didn't come to visit, her guilt was even worse. Her own mother, who had stayed by her, even after her father had banned Isabel from the family home!

Isabel's leadership experience so far was just no help in this situation. She knew that her own strengths and resources were limited. As long as her mother needed special nursing care, she could see no way at all of creating peace for herself. Well, tomorrow she was heading off to the third leadership retreat. Maybe a miracle would happen there and she would find out exactly what she should do in this hopeless situation.

The third retreat began in the rain. But while there was an incessant drizzle outside the event room, warm laughter bounced off the walls inside. An excited, happy energy pervaded the room as tribe members laughed, hugged, and greeted each other after being apart for months. This cheerful energy began to lift Isabel's spirits. The dark cloud cover that had engulfed her heart since yesterday's visit with her mother began to break up a little. She was glad to see some of the people who came up to greet her. She almost thought of them as friends. Stella and Zeke came in arm in arm, and, after another round of hugs and greetings, they sat down in two chairs in front of the semicircle.

When everyone was finally settled, Stella began, "The last retreat was all about creating from the other person. Well, this will be a very different experience. This retreat is called 'Creating from Nothing.' That may sound daunting. However, you're about to discover how rich 'nothing' really is.

"Let me start with an apology. Look, there is a lack of words in English for one aspect of what a leader has to deal with that we'll be exploring in this retreat. So we have to call it 'the space.' In Western culture, there has been very little focus on the whole issue of 'space' in relation to leadership. We love our details and our to-do lists, our goals, our deadlines, and our targets, but we rarely soften our focus enough to pay attention to the intangible element that surrounds and encloses those objectives. So we are asking that you have some patience with us as we stumble around, trying to achieve clarity in understanding what space is all about.

"This is the place in our training where we move into unknown and untried areas. Yet we believe that what you learn in this retreat makes the difference between a not-so-great leader and an exceptional leader. We also know that mucking around with these concepts will change every one of you. You'll leave with a greater understanding of 'space' and a greater facility in working with it. That's our goal for this retreat."

Zeke then took over. "Language seems to be all about labeling 'things.' We have so many ways to talk about an apple, the plate it's sitting on, and the table that holds the plate. We have very little language that talks about the empty space that surrounds and includes all those particles of matter. We can even take out our microscopes and our Wilson cloud chambers and talk about the molecules and the atoms that make up that apple. Yet, even as we look at it under a microscope, what we mostly see there is something that we don't have much language for at all: space.

"We can look out into the universe and see stars, planets, moons, nebulae, and all the particles of the universe. We can create wonderful names, numbers, and descriptive phrases for all these particles. We can know them or desire to know them well. We create entire disciplines of science to study these particles as they move through space.

"How much language do we have for the space itself? How much do we know about the space between and all around the particles? How much language have we created to understand and name what the space is? The answer is, not very much."

Stella started walking around at the front of the room as she spoke. "Yet we are aware of energy moving in that space. We are aware of changes that happen in that space. We are aware of powerful fields of emotion and mood that seem to permeate the space, separate from any individual person or thing.

"We've all been in a room or a hall where we feel a wave of energy wash over us. All of a sudden, our surroundings are transformed from the way they were before. We can look at our neighbors in the room and see the change that came over us all as a result of that wave. It's reflected in all our eyes. We ourselves can sense these shifts in the space, even though none of our five senses gives any direct, measurable evidence of that sensing."

"Great leaders have an innate ability to sense this space," Zeke continued. "They're able to sense the emotional field, the ebb and flow of the space, as it shifts. Most importantly, they can sense their own impact on the space and then take responsibility for that impact, crafting it in a way that profoundly alters the space."

Stella said, "But most of us are so particle-focused. Oh, by the way, we are using this word *particle* to distinguish all the stuff in the space from the 'space' that surrounds it. Particles include the furniture and the walls around us, everything material, but the most important particles are usually the people in the space.

"We're quite used to seeing the particles. We usually look at what's there, rather than at what surrounds it. The truth of the matter is that, in every environment, there is more space than there are particles. But we don't ever pay attention to that.

"Just look around. Most of us see this room packed with people, and we see all the people and think it's crowded. We don't see all the space that is between, above, below, and around all of the people. We feel the 'crowdedness' in the room because of our limited perception of the space.

"We could take this same room, with the same number of people in it, and open up our awareness of the space. With very little effort or time, we could replace the sense of 'crowded' with a sense of 'plenty of room.' Right now, look up. See all that unoccupied space that extends all the way to the ceiling? This room is huge!"

She sat back down as Zeke spoke. "But space is more than volume. One reason the room might have felt crowded is because of the emotional space in the room. Feelings fill the space with a charge. If everyone else is already feeling crowded when you walk in, very soon you will begin to feel claustrophobic as well. You are a sensitive antenna. You can't help it.

"So what if we want to shift the emotional space of a room? If I were the leader trying to shift that space, I could easily exhaust myself by running around to each individual, trying to convince them to shift their perspective. 'Hey you, look up. See all that space. Okay? Good! Now you, look up. See that?' That would be quite exhausting, right?"

Stella leaned forward in her chair. "And that would be the machine gun Level Two approach we talked about before. Or I could get a microphone and very loudly get everyone's attention. Have them stop whatever they are doing and then try to control them in such a way that their perspective would change. 'All of you! Look up! Right now! See all that space! This is a spacious, uncrowded room!'"

Zeke added, "But this authoritarian approach also leads to certain burnout, especially if I care about my results. Then I have to go around checking on how I did at making it somehow 'better' for everyone. I have to check in about how I did at 'solving the crowding problem' with all the people in the room, interviewing at least a majority of the particles in the space. And after all that, well, the space may change or it may not. It may just become both crowded and annoyed."

Stella spoke up again. "We're offering another alternative. I can focus on the space itself. Instead of focusing on how to shift each of the particles, I can look at what's needed to shift the space. I can feel into my self for what urges arise that match well with what I'm noticing is needed in the space. Then I can take action that follows that urge.

"That action will succeed or fail. I sense into the space, or what we call the Level Three of the room, to find out if I succeeded. If it fails, then I'll bring my attention back to the space and again look for what's needed, and then begin my journey again. Sounds kind of mysterious, doesn't it? Well, by the end of this retreat, it won't seem mysterious to you at all.

"We want you to begin to notice your impact on the Level Three—the space around you. We're warning you ahead of time that we are going to set things up so that your normal ways of noticing your impact won't work. You know, like that trick of checking out your impact with a fellow particle, another person, by asking them for feedback."

Zeke laughed, then said, "Oh, yes, and you're not going to get away with another trick that people use. We know that people often try to fake Level Three awareness by doing a rapid-fire Level Two scan of the room. They try to 'thin-slice' a sample of the reactions in the room and do some sort of instant synthesis and analysis of what is going on in all of those quick reads on the reactions. Then they come up with a summary that they try to pass off as reading the Level Three."

Stella said, "That trick is also doomed to fail in the work we are doing this week. What often happens in this rapid-fire reading of all the Level Twos is that your attention is naturally drawn to the brightest particle or energy at Level Two. That brightness could be a reaction or judgment you are having toward someone's present- ation, or a strong reaction that one person is having, or it could be an excitement or enthusiasm you have about something or someone. The point is that while it may be an accurate read of a particle, it may have almost nothing at all to do with what's really in the space."

Zeke stood up. "No, we want you to be able to soften your focus and to train yourself to sense around you—all 360 degrees around you. We want you to imagine yourself as a pebble dropped into the middle of a pond. There are ripples radiating out from your impact, heading to the edges of that pond. Now imagine you can actually feel those ripples moving across the surface of the pond. And now feel the first ripples reaching the edges. We want to train you to feel the journey of those ripples of your impact through the pond, and to feel the contact of the ripples with the edges of the pond."

"Exactly," said Stella. "Your brain is going to want to do the habitual thing of hard-focusing on the journey of the pebble as it hits the water and sinks to the bottom, rather than focusing on the ripples in the water. We are going to have to give that part of the brain a little vacation as you explore this different way of sensing."

Zeke held his hand, palm up, toward Stella. "Take this pebble from my hand, Grasshopper."

Stella ended the session with, "So this retreat, above all others, will challenge you and mess with your brain and your normal way of doing things. For some of you, that will be a joyful experience. For others of you, it may be uncomfortable. So what else is new?"

Nervous laughter rippled through the room.

Isabel had been rooming with Emily since the first retreat. They had gotten along easily, in a friendly and not-too-intimate way that worked well for Isabel. So she was a little surprised to find herself in a fight with Emily on the very first afternoon of the retreat. It started when Emily started talking about her Leadership Quest.

"You know, in the last retreat, when they told us we had to create a Leadership Quest, some big project to change the world, I just couldn't get behind that whole idea for months. I remember you complaining about it, too, on our last tribe call. But then, last weekend, I was going through my old photographs, and I found my high school yearbook. There I was in so many pictures, trying to stand behind someone else. I've been battling weight issues my whole life. I remembered how painful it was to be an overweight adolescent, and then suddenly I had it.

"Despite the recent spate of articles and programs about teenage obesity, our society is still judging larger girls and making them wrong somehow. So I decided I want to take a stand, to create a program in high school for supporting teenagers to accept their bodies instead of hating them. I want girls to feel okay about how they look, instead of starving and taking drugs to try to morph their shape into something pixie-like and unattainable.

"Since then, it's been almost as if the universe has been waiting for me to create these self-image workshops. All sorts of resources and co-collaborators are coming out of the woodwork to help. It is a bit magical. Something outside of me seems to be guiding all this. My guides are working overtime."

That was when Isabel lost it. "Oh, I don't think I can stand another minute of this New Age, pebble-in-the-pond, law-of-attraction, light-energy, shift-the-space, higher-power, universal-magic bullshit. The universe doesn't give a damn about your project. It's much too busy spinning itself toward uniform entropy.

"Look, Emily, there's a straight line of irrational, patriarchal, and ultimately demeaning thought that runs right through Western history, from John Calvin to Tony Robbins, saying, 'Work hard and get God's blessing. Think and grow rich, or grow healthy, or grow happily married. Imagine it, and it's yours!' That crap completely ignores real human suffering. Work can still be demeaning, and devastating shit can still happen to anyone, anytime.

"I work every day with people who are mangled, disfigured, shattered by accidents and illness, and sometimes just by being born. And if that isn't enough, all I have to do is look at my mother's face when she forgets what a paper straw is for. Don't tell me 'God doesn't give us more than we can handle'! I know differently."

Isabel was a little surprised by the vehemence of her reaction, but she was stunned when the formerly meek Emily came right back at her. "Hey, surprise! There might be a possibility that you do not understand everything there is to know about the workings of the universe, Isabel. I think you know me better than to think I am naïve.

"I'm a therapist, for Christ's sake. I've seen inexplicable human suffering. And yet there is still something I can't quite logically explain about how remarkable it has been that resources have tumbled into my lap since last Saturday, when I set my Stake. I just can't write it off as coincidence or good luck. Hey, I'm not arrogant enough to think it's all because Jesus loves me. But it isn't as simple as you want to make it out to be. The universe may contain more to it than entropy. Sorry that you don't agree, but for me it still seems a bit miraculous."

Isabel wasn't letting go. "Look, I can see you are having some sort of unusual experience. But until something like that happens to me, all I can say is that I am chewing on a big grain of salt about this 'tune in to the space' stuff. I don't think this retreat is going to be a lot of fun for me."

As she spoke, everything felt bristly, like she was rooming with a porcupine. If this was sensing the space, it sucked. She walked out of the room and blindly followed the path down to the dusty road. She knew she would eventually turn around, but right now it felt good just to be walking away.

During **dinner** that evening, Isabel watched as Phil passed his iPhone around, showing everyone the pictures of his new baby daughter. The other women in the room were all cooing. For the thousandth time, she wondered if there was something broken inside her. She just wasn't into infants, kids, or the whole maternal thing. Okay, her sister's son was kind of cute and had a nice smile. But she didn't melt when she held him, and she just couldn't get excited at the sight of someone else's little Winston Churchill–looking newborn.

Violet was a natural at all that stuff. But Isabel felt much more like the guys who looked at the pictures, said, "Cool, very pretty girl," and looked around for the coffeepot before extricating themselves from the henhouse. Except for Allen, of course, who was clucking along with the best of them. Behind her superficial smile, she felt empty inside. If this was creating from nothing, it was going to be a very disappointing week.

Then she caught Olivia's eye. Standing on the other side of the crowd that clustered around Phil's iPhone, Olivia looked at Allen, then at Isabel, and then rolled her eyes. Hmm, maybe she wasn't so alone in this after all.

The rain fell softly as Isabel sat in "her place," right next to a redwood, on a stump that provided her with a comfortable, natural chair. It was well off the path, overlooking a pocket valley covered with more redwoods. She'd found it on the first retreat, and it had stayed her secret place ever since. She liked being somewhere where no one could find her. Today she was going to be there for several hours, doing one of the "in silence" assigned exercises. She was trying to look beyond the details of what was around her and to see the space, the air around every particle. She was feeling rather bored and getting pretty grumpy.

There was a branch hanging down in front of her. She began to let her eyes rest on one of its pointed edges. From time to time, a drop of water fell from it to the ground. She just sat there, watching drop after drop fall.

Then she began trying to watch the space around the drop as it became swollen, ready to fall. As she watched the space that contained it, each drop became unique, three-dimensional, and vibrant. Then something even more unusual began to happen. She became aware of sitting in the same space that the drop was swelling in. Her focus shifted from a hard focus on the drop to a softer focus that included the drop, the branch, the view of the valley through the branches, and an awareness of her body and the space around her as she watched the drops form and fall.

It was hard to find words for this experience, but it was as though a filter had dropped away. Her awareness expanded, and now she could see in more dimensions than before. And something was relaxing inside her as this happened. "This is weird," she said to the next drop that was forming.

As she sat in a circle in the group room, waiting for the debriefing to begin, Isabel did not want to speak. She didn't want to analyze what was going on inside her, and besides, she couldn't really put it into words. So instead of sharing, she just listened.

Phil said, "This stuff is weird. I was sitting on a log. Somehow I managed to find a dry spot, and sorry, but I was thinking more about a big sales meeting coming up than about the space. Then I started hearing the rain. It was barely perceptible, the lightest sound. But I slowed down my breathing and just listened.

"And here is the weird thing. As I just sat there, no longer thinking about anything, a gray fox stepped out into a clearing just below me and looked up at me. Suddenly, I had this great idea about the sales meeting, and how I could use a story that my client had told me to frame the presentation. And I swear, the fox barked at me and scurried off. Have you trained the wildlife around here as assistant leaders or something?"

Many in the group laughed. But Isabel didn't. She just looked at Phil and saw that, underneath his humor, he had also been touched by something he couldn't quite put words to.

Stella interrupted their laughter. "Phil, I have a startling idea for you, so hold on to your hat. Notice that just having a thought shifted the Level Three of the space that contained you and the fox. And Mr. Fox was a wonderful barometer of that shift. He moved when he sensed a change in the Level Three, when the ripple of the thought went through the space and hit the fox. When you make an impact on the Level Three, something changes.

"The particle of Phil didn't move a muscle, or change its expression, or create any other physical cue for Mr. Fox to leave. Yet something changed in the impact you were having. And the only thing you were aware of changing was your thought. The fox wasn't reading your mind. He didn't all of a sudden realize that he wasn't interested in that subject. No, the fox was aware of a shift in the space that you created by shifting your focus of energy, and he moved in response."

Zeke added, "You are always having an impact on the space. Most of the time we are completely unconscious of what that impact is, and we just keep thinking, saying, and doing things, unaware that every thought, change in facial muscles, gesture, action, word we say has an impact on the Level Three. That's one of the outcomes of this retreat: to open up your awareness of your impact on the space, to notice the shifts that occur in the space when you act this way or that way.

"At first it's important to just notice it. Don't worry about it or try to change it or take responsibility for it. All that will come later. Right now, just notice. And be grateful for the barometers that other people, and other animals, provide as feedback about your impact on the space."

Isabel's old objections to this leadership approach suddenly bubbled up. She couldn't just sit here like a compliant child, listening to all this bullshit. She exploded, "Look, I see most of the people in this room nodding and smiling. That's just swell for them. After all, we are in California. But what good is all this transpersonal-space language and silent-meditation crap when I am sitting in front of a room full of rich East Coast donors who are tapped out and not feeling particularly philanthropic, or when I am arguing with a union organizer in one of my board-and-care facilities? I think you're leaving the real world far behind you in this retreat."

Zeke smiled. "Isabel, I promise to address how to use what we are teaching, in real-world settings, before the end of this retreat. But right now I want to look at a more general issue related to the one you brought up. You called it 'transpersonal-space language' and 'silent-meditation crap.'

"Part of the language challenge that we face when we try to talk about the Level Three or the space is that a lot of the language has been usurped by religions and the New Age movement. It seems that trouble happens when we use terms from the language that the personal-growth, spiritual folk have adopted. We risk alienating a whole bunch of people—like you, Isabel—who don't use that language in their daily lives, and who can, in fact, get quite reactive when language like that shows up.

"It's not only our language that has gotten twisted around and associated with certain disciplines. It's also practices like meditation, visualization, contemplation, sitting in stillness in nature, and so many others that help to soften the focus in such a way that you actually enter the space or the nothingness. These practices support you in becoming more aware of things like the Level Three, the space, and the invisible energy field surrounding everything. Those terms and practices are so non-secular that even mentioning them will take all of your minds to familiar and potentially reactive places. Some of you will smile, feeling right at home. Some will frown, feeling that we just left the real world. But you will all react.

"As we use the language of these disciplines and practices, we are sure to offend some of your sensibilities and cause some alienating reactions in some of you. So, Isabel, I ask that you notice this and move past your reactions. I hear your concern, and I'm asking you to let go of your judging mind a bit as we attempt to explore this vast mystery. Just for now, and just for a few days, let go of memories of rooms full of stingy donors or disgruntled union reps, and take this journey with us. This is a time just for you to begin to notice the distinctions between your focus on the particles and your focus on the space. Join us in this experiment. Let yourself become more and more aware of the space. Begin to notice the impact of your own energy on that space."

Isabel shrugged. "Sure, I'll give it a shot. So how do I do that?"

Zeke asked, "So, what do you notice about your impact on the space in this room right now?"

Isabel paused. "Well, inside I am prickly. But the room seems attentive and not very riled up by what I said."

Zeke said, "Yes, I noticed that, too. It's almost as if this were the additional element that was needed to balance out our proselytizing. A good, healthy skepticism will benefit all our learning, and you get to carry that for us."

Stella said, "Isabel asked, 'How can I do that?' Well, that is a good question. I don't know how you yourself will learn how to sense and impact the space, Isabel. All we can do is give you some exercises that we know can open up your awareness and point you in the right direction. You're going to start building 'muscles' that will help you get better at this noticing.

"But you will have to find your own answer to the question 'How?' 'How does my being here impact the space?' 'What if I do this or say that?' 'How does the space change?' We want you to simply notice and not judge or attempt to change your impact at first. We want you to take risks and step into new and different ways of being. Then notice the impact of that on the space. We want you to be yourselves, with all of your messy reactions, and notice the impact of that on the space. We want you to be as non-judgmental as possible."

Isabel noticed that her arms were still crossed. But she knew her apparent indifference was a little false. There was a bittersweet irony to all this. Stella and Zeke wanted her to go into the empty space and hang out while her mother was fighting like hell to get out of her own empty spaces, and losing that fight more and more with every day that passed.

For the next exercise, they watched a video segment of a stand-up comedian relating the story of a disastrous date. As he dryly related one catastrophe after another, the room kept bursting into laughter. He ended by saying, "So there I stood in the pouring rain, pants down around my knees, my arm in a cast, a rash breaking out on my neck. I decided nothing could get worse. So that was when I asked her to marry me."

After the laughter died down and Stella turned off the video, Zeke began. "Lots of fun, but entertainment wasn't why we showed you this clip. What we want you to notice is how this guy managed time and content to build his routine. One crucial thing that exists in the space is time and its first cousin, timing. When we say, 'She's got a great sense of timing' or, 'He's got a feel for the rhythm,' what are we talking about? It seems that one of the ways we can have an impact on the space is with our awareness of the timing of things.

"Timing is crucial to being responsible for your impact. Timing is something that you can feel if you are paying attention. Great leaders have an innate understanding of this, and they design what they do or say with the right timing. The right timing is a pace that is perfectly aligned with the needs of the space and is also matched to their own rhythms."

Stella picked it up. "Let's start with your breath. For most of us, it's perfectly timed with a natural arc or rhythm. We inhale to a certain natural place of having the 'right' amount of air, and then we naturally exhale until we get to a place somewhere near the bottom, but not at the bottom, and then we naturally take in the next breath. This natural arc of timing is set deep within us, and every cell in our body knows when the timing is right and when it's off. Working a room can use that same awareness."

She must have become aware of the confusion in the space. Or maybe she just saw all the blank stares. "Okay, let me come at this from another angle. Every movie, every story, has an arc. Let's create a sci-fi film, *The Last Mission of the SS* Phoenix. Our intrepid space explorers start off from Earth, all hopeful and happy. That is the beginning of the arc.

"Then their faster-than-light-speed drive breaks down, they crash on a planet, the lovers get separated and one of them may have died, dinosaurs chase them around, and so on. Each event is worse than the last. The arc is building. Finally, the few remaining survivors are hanging in the web of the giant, carnivorous, super-intelligent Spider Queen. Now we're at the top of the arc, one hour and fifty minutes into the film.

"In the next ten minutes, they will be rescued, the lovers will be reunited, and the Spider Queen will end up with a spear in her craw, and the last thing we'll see will be the heroes in a life ship heading back to Earth. That is a completed arc. Note that it's not symmetrical—there was a long, bumpy rise and a rapid fall—but it's still complete and satisfying to the audience." She saw the nods and heard the murmurs of understanding around the room.

She continued, "Now, let's go back to our discussion about breathing. If we hold our breath too long at the top or force out every bit of air at the bottom, it's unnatural. We call that *arcus prolongus*. If we pant and cut the breath short before we reach the top or the bottom, and quickly move in the other direction, it also feels unnatural. We call that *arcus interruptus*.

"In that comedy clip about the date from purgatory, we saw how the comic played with the arc, stretching it out during the automobile accident, hurrying through the story of the emergency room at the hospital, orchestrating time and timing to build to the scene in the poison-ivy patch."

Zeke said, "When we don't pay attention to the timing that exists in the space, we can make one of two fatal errors. We can throw in way too much detail or content and bore the space and our audience. We soon notice their eyes glazing over, and that many of them are trying to stifle their yawns. That's a bad case of *arcus prolongus*. Or we can frustrate the Level Three with *arcus interruptus*, rushing to make our very important points and blind to the fact that we have left everyone far behind us.

"Great stories and symphonies unfold with a timing that is as ingrained in our cells as our breath. They build naturally to a climax and then descend to a resolution. There are variations of this natural arc of time, but for the most part, we have been telling stories and playing music that follows this sense of timing for as long as we have been able to communicate with each other. We keep our audience engaged and inspired by how we fill in that arc."

Stella continued, "Except that most of the so-called 'leaders' in our lives don't engage us with their stories the same way. Instead, they are clueless about the arc, always busy stringing together beads of this fact and that opinion and either boring or frustrating us."

Zeke added, "What would the world be like if its leaders engaged us like a great story or a symphony? If they kept us inspired to follow along so we couldn't wait to see how it all turns out? That new kind of leader has an impeccable sense of timing. He or she knows how to keep the space interested, and knows when it's time to start a new story. All of that comes from noticing what is happening in the space and being responsible for it."

After dinner that evening, everyone was quieter than usual. Emily was sitting in her usual place next to the fire, writing in her journal about the day's events. Allen and Phil were next to the piano, talking intently. Isabel sat apart from the others. She had a lot to think about and wasn't interested in making nice, social conversation. She watched the rain tracking its way down the windows and wondered how her mother was doing right now.

Suddenly, she noticed two male voices becoming tense. Phil and Allen were arguing over religion, and the argument was getting heated. At first she wanted to jump in on Phil's side. But then an even more interesting idea hit her. *Let's run a little trial test on all this impact-the-space crap,* she mused to herself. *If I assume that I have an impact on the space, then I wonder what positive impact I could have on their conversation. How could I shift the con-versation without them even knowing it? So what kind of space do I want to create? Let's see if this BS really works.*

She moved over to their table and asked, "Do you mind if I just listen in? It sounds like a lively debate!"

"Sure."

"No problem."

The two guys made room for her and then went right back at each other. Phil was saying, "But, Allen, how can you devote yourself to a church that has been responsible for so much bloodshed and intolerance and now seems to be polarizing the country into extremes?"

Allen answered, "You really know very little about the impact churches are having on our culture these days, because it doesn't make for dramatic, conflict-ridden news stories. All the crackpots get on CNN, while millions of gentle Christians are making this world a better place to live in."

Now Isabel felt it was time for her experiment. She sat up in her chair. How could her energy make things worse? Could she pollute the space without saying anything? First, she imagined the two of them getting into a fistfight. She held that image fiercely in her mind as she watched them argue. She became aware of the tension on her face as she focused on them.

Allen was saying, "Look, I'm Episcopalian, not Catholic, so stop blaming me for the Inquisition."

Phil jumped right back in. "But any time you leave the world of reason and intelligence and head off into unquestioned faith and obedience, which is where every church wants you to be, then you are creating the space for another Inquisition."

This was working almost too well. Isabel wondered if she could intend an opposite impact. Could she shift the space without stepping in to break them up? She sat back and took a deep, long breath and let her forehead relax. She began imagining Phil and Allen agreeing to disagree. She saw a picture of them shaking hands. She let a smile emerge at the ends of her mouth.

Phil was saying, "But you can't just turn your back on a thousand years' history of religious tyranny!"

Allen replied, "You're right—of course I can't do that. But where do I want to take a stand? Do I just turn my back on the church and give up, or am I willing to travel a riskier road and try to change it?"

Phil turned to Isabel. "I see you're wearing a crucifix. You're Catholic, right?" Startled to be drawn into her own experiment, Isabel nodded.

Phil said, "So, does either one of you really think that a huge church like the Catholics or the Episcopalians can be changed by people like us?"

Isabel shrugged and smiled, still envisioning them shaking each other's hands.

Allen said, "I don't know if we can or not. But I know I'm called upon to try. I'd welcome any ideas about where I might start, Phil."

Phil said, "Oh, like I'm going to be able to do that? Right!"

Isabel couldn't contain herself. By now, she was really interested. So she said, "Why not you?"

Phil laughed. "Okay, let's take a crack at changing the past two thousand years of religious tradition. So, what do you want to change first, Allen?"

Allen said, "Boy, that's easy. My bishop. He is turning into Torquemada."

Phil said, "Well, you know, I was working with that pain-in-the-ass manager I told you about last retreat. When we were together at our workshop, Isabel used that Acceptance-Alignment-Under-standing-Agreement model on him and me. It actually worked, didn't it, Isabel?" He looked over at her, and she nodded. Then he turned back to Allen.

"Tell me about your torturer, and maybe Isabel and I can help you see how to apply it."

Isabel was a tiny bit disturbed by this change of energy and direction. Either this was one hell of a coincidence or maybe this stuff actually worked, even if she couldn't figure out how.

While the retreat was structured to give the participants a lot of time to reflect, Isabel found it was both a blessing and a curse. She certainly needed the quiet and the space to come to terms with all the changes that were happening in her life, especially her mother's rapid deterioration. But having this time also brought up a lot of emotions, particularly a sense of grief about the loss of her mother's love, that she didn't know how to deal with.

But the days were not the worst times. Isabel prided herself on being a healthy sleeper, but in this retreat her sleep was a mess. Most nights, she tossed and turned, trying to settle down, and then woke up in the dark, shaken by her dreams. One night she felt as though she'd spent the whole night searching for her mother through their apartment but found only traces of her. Finally, the phone rang in her dream. It was *Mamita Luisa*, and she was annoyed.

"Isabel, stop stomping around up there. I am trying to sleep. You sound like *un elefante*. Step lightly, Isabel!"

Isabel had woken up and could not get back to sleep.

The next morning, Isabel was intensely restless during the silent journaling time that preceded the first session. She just couldn't settle down. She was about to jump out of her skin. As she was squirming in her chair, trying to find a comfortable position, it finally hit her. It wasn't about her dream. It had to do with the group and this retreat.

She actually had a very interesting story to tell about shifting the space in the room the prior evening, but she wasn't ready to share it. Until now, she had thought of her role in this tribe as that of a resident realist among a band of New Age dreamers—a very familiar role for her. But today she wasn't feeling like the naysayer. This stuff really might be true. And she didn't want to let on that she was getting converted.

Luckily, it turned out that she didn't need to speak, because Zeke started addressing the issue almost as though he were responding to her unvoiced story. He said, "I've been thinking about how to describe a particular aspect of the skill of orienting toward the space of a room or a situation. It has to do with orienting to the emotional field of the room.

"Have you ever experienced really feeling terrific—joyful, actually; in a great mood—and you walk into a room where the air itself feels thick with grief, sadness, or anger? It is clear that you weren't feeling that way at all before, and all of a sudden there is a very different emotion all around you.

"You look into the room, and you don't necessarily find the "source" of that anger or grief in one individual, and yet you can clearly feel it in the space around you. As you look around the room at other individuals, you might see them in that emotion or reflecting it, or you might see faces of confusion or bewilderment, because these people are also clearly feeling something that wasn't generated from their emotions. It might be something they also walked into.

"We're amazingly sensitive creatures. Not every emotion that we feel comes from our emotional self. Sometimes we can take on the emotions of another person. And when we walk into a space that is filled with a different emotion, we can often take on that emotion as our own.

"When we can separate our emotional life from those other emotional realities that can swirl around us, then we can begin to notice our ability to have an impact on that emotional field. When we can begin to notice that impact, we then can begin to take responsibility for that impact and to shift it or strengthen it."

As Isabel looked around the room, she noticed the attention being paid to every word that Zeke spoke. She began to realize just how true it was for her, just as much as it was for the others, that she did actually react to the space around her. She just hadn't been aware of it before now.

When Isabel walked into the event room that afternoon, she groaned. This was not going to be fun! It was the Web, an exercise she had done years ago in a management development seminar. A frame six feet tall and fifteen feet wide had thin strings slung across it to define about twenty oddly-shaped, empty spaces. Little bells hung from many of the strings. The object of the exercise was for everyone to pass from one side of the frame to the other, through the "holes" defined by the strings, without anyone touching any string or the frame. When she had tried it back then, her team had failed dismally. Every time a string got touched, a bell would tinkle, and everyone had to come back and start again.

Her déjà vu got worse. This exercise was going exactly like that other one had. Phil stepped in and started organizing everybody, just as she had done years ago. Breakdown ahead! This time, she was going to just shut up. At least it wouldn't be her fault when they failed this time.

People's failures and frustrations were mounting. Every time a string was touched, everyone who had already made it through to the other side had to walk back around and start again. Allen and Phil began to argue. Isabel waited silently for Stella and Zeke to give up on them and announce the end of this futile exercise.

Eventually, Stella did step in. "All right, have you had enough of leadership the way you always experienced it before?" Everyone groaned and nodded.

She went on, "Remember, this is a retreat about space. About the malleability and flexibility of space. You're all fixated on the

particles, including your bodies and the strings, making sure that
no one touches them. Focusing obsessively on the obstacle is
leading you all toward a spectacular failure. Debating strategies to
manage the particles more efficiently only creates more chaos. Has
everyone had enough?"

There was a chorus of "Yes!"

"So, here are two new rules and a hint. Rule number one: no
more speaking, period. If anyone speaks, everyone begins again.
Rule number two: all the big holes on the lowest row are now
closed. You may use the one small hole on the first row only once.
From then on, you can use only the holes in rows two, three, and
four. You can use the second- and third-row holes only twice each.
Now, here's your hint: focus on the space. Open the space, stretch
it, and you will all get through. Breathe and begin."

The tribe began by forming a circle and standing for a moment
in silence. Isabel felt the return of that calm she had discovered in
the forest on the second day and noticed how she started to
reconnect with the other people in the room. It wasn't about not
being responsible for the failure. It was about playing her part in
the victory! Then people gravitated over toward one of the holes.
Phil raised his hand, and two of them lifted his legs. He walked on
his hands through to the other side as they eased his legs through
the hole. It was graceful and moving.

Which didn't mean that they didn't have to start again. Several
times, in fact. Once, they were nearly all through, and were putting
Isabel through a high hole, when a string was touched and a bell
tinkled. Everyone silently hugged in a big circle. Then they went
back over to the side where they'd started and peacefully began
again. No longer were there pushy leaders or people standing aside,
waiting for something to happen. Each person found a role. And
that role was always changing as more and more people went
through the web. Isabel noticed something strange. Just as Stella
had advised them, she began looking at the spaces, instead of at the
strings, and they did seem to magically expand.

In what turned out to be the successful round, Emily smiled, pointed to a small, very high, triangular-shaped space, and then pointed to herself. Isabel shook her head. Emily was a large woman, and there was no way she was going to fit through that tiny hole. But by now, Emily had already been lifted off the ground. Everyone was smiling. As improbable as it looked, they knew that they could do this. They turned Emily sideways, and almost effortlessly, she slid through the hole and was caught by the group on the other side. Emily had tears in her eyes when they gently laid her on the ground. There were unexpected tears in Isabel's eyes, too. *That was so beautiful*, she thought.

Isabel was so focused on helping everyone get through the web that she was quite surprised to find herself the last one left on her side. How on earth was she going to get off the ground and through the last legal hole by herself? As she looked at the web, she had to shake her head and remind herself to focus on the space, not on the strings. As she put her arms and shoulders into the space, she felt herself held by some of the people on the other side. She arched her back and let them pull her gently through. No string was touched, and no bell tinkled. Unicorns victorious! Finally, the room erupted with cheers, whistles, and back-slapping.

Olivia led off the debriefing. "I couldn't stand Phil and Allen's Testosterone School of Leadership that started this exercise. They were right out of the fifties. 'Anyone entrusted with power will abuse it.'"

Isabel had heard it all before and was starting to space out. But she was right back when Zeke snapped, "Olivia, knock it off."

Stella stepped in. "Olivia, I know this is a hot button for you, but what impact are you having in the room right now by starting the debriefing with this?"

Olivia said, "I've just had enough of men abusing their power just because . . ."

Zeke stood up and in a loud voice said, "Stop! This is an old story for you, isn't it, Olivia? Men suck!"

The room tensed up. Then he said, "In the web, you kept trying to crawl through on your own and you kept failing miserably. Tell the truth now, Miss Sex Type. It felt good to be lifted up and safely held by those guys, didn't it?"

Olivia glared at him. Then she smiled. "Yep, it really did." The room broke up.

Stella went on, "So, all of you practiced two ways of moving through space in this exercise: focusing on the strings and focusing on the space between the strings.

"One way was much more successful than the other one. Most of us humans spend most of our lives running around, wanting everyone to get out of our way while we're making sure we don't bump into anybody or anything else. Or we push ourselves and everyone else to do things our way. As you discovered, the faster we move around through life and the more we try to control it, the more we end up bumping into things, bouncing off of people and particles. We spend our time careering through life, trying so hard not to get caught up in the particles, focusing on the strings, as it were, that we end up getting trapped in them.

"Then you tried something else. As a group, you shifted your focus from the particles of the strings toward an awareness of the spaces between them, and you were able to get everyone through the web. Think about the implications. What if, instead of moving from barrier to barrier in our lives, we moved into spaces, and then moved into more spaces again? Then, instead of avoiding particles, in every move we made we would find more space to move into. We need to let go of the old beliefs we had about space and time and what is or isn't possible. What if we could still always find the space in front of us? What is amazing is that when we do that, even if all the circumstances are the same, we end up not bumping into the particles at all."

Zeke stepped in. "Exactly. For me, there are two metaphors that I think demonstrate this most powerfully in my own life: skiing among trees and riding a motorcycle around a sharp curve. When you're skiing through trees, you want to be sure to look at the space where you want to ski, and not at the trees. The minute you look at a tree, you smash into it. When you're on a motorcycle going around a sharp curve, you want to keep your eyes focused on the open road ahead of you as you move through the curve. As soon as your eyes glance at the ditch over on the side of the road, in the next instant you are in that ditch.

"The same is true for moving through our lives. If we focus on all the problems that need to be solved and all the fires that need putting out, all we keep doing is putting out fires and solving problems. We can get very good at this and yet feel completely trapped by it as well. That is exactly what your group was doing before we stopped you. But when you can focus on the spaces between those fires, the context that surrounds all those little problems, you'll be able to move in ways that allow you to be much more flexible and agile. You'll know without thinking just what is needed to keep things moving and how to manage whatever comes at you. And sometimes that process allows us to create beautiful moments."

At **dinner** that night, Isabel went over to Zeke's table.

"I just need to say that when you yelled at Olivia in group, that was completely uncalled for. It was exactly the kind of bullish, authoritarian, testosterone-laced approach that I thought leadership was supposed to supplant."

Zeke said, "You know, that old habit of seeing all males as unfeeling bozos may be getting in your way of seeing clearly."

Isabel came right back: "Actually, you are doing to me right now exactly what you were doing to Olivia earlier."

When Zeke opened his mouth to reply, he felt a hand on his shoulder. He looked up. It was Stella. She said, "Isabel, you have a very legitimate concern. You want to know what was happening in the room that created the urge for Zeke to do what he did."

Zeke said, "I want to respond to you, Isabel, and I think everyone else should hear. There are two very important things about what you brought up. Are you willing to wait an hour to hear what I want to say?"

In a slightly sarcastic tone, Isabel replied, "Sure, I'm looking forward to it."

Zeke stood up and said, "Hello, everyone. Attention, please! A couple of people have mentioned their concerns about something that happened today. I want us all to meet for a short session this evening, right after dinner, to address it. Then the rest of the night will be free time."

After dinner, everyone was seated back in the event room, with a feeling of expectancy and anticipation.

Zeke began, "Isabel was upset about my interactions with Olivia today, and she came to me to tell me. I'm guessing there was a disturbance in the space. True?" A number of people nodded.

"I am glad she came to me. It gives us an opportunity to look at two dynamic lessons that are critical to leadership. First of all, Olivia, the complete quotation that you gave us a fragment of today was written by Jean de La Fontaine. It goes, 'Anyone entrusted with power will abuse it if not also animated with the love of truth and virtue, no matter whether he be a prince, or one of the people.' I know this quotation well, because it was one of my ex-lover's favorite weapons to throw at me when he thought I was being a jerk. And when I told you to knock it off, I was in one hundred percent reaction mode. I wasn't seeing you at all, only him. My skillful co-leader jumped right in without making me wrong. She broke in and took charge of moving the focus away from me and back to you. So, lesson number one: sometimes you lose it as a leader, and a co-leader whom you trust can save your neck.

"A few moments later, I stood up and yelled at you again. This, however, was not because of any reaction I was having. Which brings us to lesson two. Leaders are not always 'nice.' All of you need to see that situation through my eyes. It had very little to do with Olivia and everything to do with the needs of the space. As a leader, I'm almost always aware of and responsible for the space." The room laughed at his facial expression as he said "almost."

Zeke went on, "I pay some attention to what is happening in the space. Sometimes it may look like I am just focused on working with one individual and his or her particular issue in a very focused, Level Two way. But in fact, I am actually working the space *through* that individual.

"In my second interaction with Olivia, I saw that she was still intensely wrapped up in her story. But as I opened my focus, I also became aware that the room was falling asleep a bit. Now, I could have followed her energy and really focused on her with Level Two attention and worked on that issue about her and men's power. I would have eventually gotten somewhere with her. However, I would have lost the room. So, while I might have been helping Olivia, I wasn't leading.

"This is going to be a tricky concept for some of you who work as consultants, problem-solvers, therapists, or coaches to wrap your brain around. The temptation in you is to focus in hard on the one with the problem. One-on-one focus is almost an addiction. You rarely ask yourself, 'What is everyone needing right now in the room?' Instead you serve the one, sometimes at the expense of the many. That is why paying attention to the space will be such a radical idea for you.

"Now, my Stake for every interaction in this retreat is to create from the space. I need to be aware of my impact on the space and then create from it. So I cranked up my emotion and my volume, probably a bit more than was necessary, to get Olivia's attention. I cranked it up that loud in order to get everyone else's wandering attention as well.

"The space in the room snapped right back to attention; some of you were even awake enough to form judgments and/or projections about the way I was responding to Olivia. I completely trusted Olivia and knew that we could repair anything that needed repairing if I went too far.

"It also wasn't very important to me whether or not I created reactions in other individuals in the room. I know and trust that if I'm oriented toward the Stake, and I stay aware of and responsible for the impact that I want to have in the space, then I will eventually be able to take care of any individual reactions. I trust that anyone who needs to work things out with me will come up to me and clear what is going on for them, just like Isabel did at dinner tonight."

Stella joined in. "So, even when we are working with one person, our focus is on the space and the Stake. I am always working through the individual whom I am having the dialogue with in order to impact both the individual and the space we all inhabit—both the person and the space, not either/or. Sometimes the content of the dialogue is less important to the Stake that I am holding than what is occurring in the space in that moment."

Zeke said, "Yes, I am more interested in whether the room is confused or frustrated than in whether any individuals are. I have to stop and clarify things only when I feel the room is lost. My primary responsibility as a leader is to the space and to the Leader Stake in any given moment. When I forget that, I can get pulled into the particles, like Olivia's particular issue with the web, and get pulled off the Stake. Then leadership leaves the room.

"For those of you who are professional helpers in any capacity, including managers and parents, this is going to be really hard to get used to. You'll be drawn to doing the intense one-on-one work like a moth to the flame. Disaster. If you learn nothing else in this retreat, learn this: you have to give your primary attention to the space, and only secondarily to the individual; otherwise, you are going to go down in flames. Right, Olivia?"

Olivia smiled as she said, "Zeke, you were a real dick. For a moment I thought, *This is just what I'm talking about: another example of men pushing their weight around.* But then I listened to you. You were right. I did like all those big guys gently manhandling me. Then I realized you were right about the other thing, too. I was just whining again about an old story, when, actually, that whole web event was pretty magical for me. My old story was tanking the room after what was an amazing event. So I just let go and trusted you had a good reason for doing what you did. Thanks for fleshing out that reason for us."

Isabel thought to herself, *I think I might have been wrong about Zeke. I assumed he was being just another male jerk. He's definitely a male, but maybe not such a jerk.*

Down in the staff room that evening, Stella toasted Zeke with a cup of hot cocoa. "Great save tonight."

"Stella, Stella, Stella. You so covered my ass today. I was snapping away at Olivia, and then I did it all over again with Isabel."

Stella smiled back at him. "Thanks. Any time. But actually, I'm a little ticked off at you. You never lose it like that. So what's really going on?"

Zeke sighed. "I had another bad call with Jason last night. Damn, if I didn't take it out on the Unicorns. I'm sorry. I guess I screwed up."

Stella took his hand. "Look, I am sorry about you and Jason. But this snapping needs to stop. And I mean right now! I appreciated your being real about your reactions in front of the group tonight. That was a good moment for them, seeing that sometimes we fail, too. But we are on a damn important retreat. They need all of you. So I am making a request of you. Please stop calling Jason while you're here on this retreat. Don't talk to him at all. No texts, no tweets, no Facebook messages—nothing. We don't need a replay of tonight. I need you fully here, not heartbroken, and not with your attention split in half."

Zeke looked down and then back up, into her eyes. "You're right to be angry. I agree. No more Jason. No more spoiling the space. I'm back here with you now."

It was the evening before the last day of the third retreat. Small groups were forming and dissolving as people chatted or made plans for staying in touch until the next retreat. At dinner, Isabel had enjoyed a spirited conversation with Olivia about how repulsive most babies looked. Now she was sitting alone by the fireplace, reading an interesting book of haiku she had found on a shelf in the retreat center library. It was an odd volume, with one black-and-white photograph on each page. Each picture was covered with a haiku, printed on a translucent overlay.

She kept turning back to the page that had a picture of an abandoned shack and a haiku that read:

Sold the house,
Closed the cabin,
I am moving into the empty room.

It reminded her of her life right now. As her mother faded away rapidly, a whole chapter of her life as a daughter was ending. It felt as if her childhood home were being sold. It felt though her own life were turning into another translucent overlay. She could feel a chill, because she was sure her life was about to change in other, as yet unknown ways.

Allen came over and sat next to her. "Got a minute, Isabel?"

"Lots of them." She closed her book. "What's up?"

"Oh, I was just wondering how this retreat was for you. I remember before it started, you said something like you were afraid that this leadership program was all optimistic, naïve California, Pollyanna fluff. Just wondering if that opinion has changed any."

Isabel paused. She searched for the right words. Then she just sat in the silence, waiting for the words to find her. Finally she said, "It was harder than I thought it was going to be. I've had some rough patches this week. There's a lot going on in my personal life, and having so much time just with myself brought all that stuff into the spotlight.

"I realized that I was impacting others around me, especially my roommate, unintentionally impacting her in a really negative way. If I want to lead and empower people, I'd better be intentional about that impact. At the ritual we held at the end of the second retreat, we had this delicious wave of affection for each other. It touched me, but some part of me didn't exactly trust it. But the workshop I did with Phil after the second retreat was so powerful that I started to trust in this leadership process. And in this retreat, I got to see things about how to shift energy in the room that I never fully understood before. I have to say, this work is deeper and more foundationally challenging than I thought it was going to be.

"So, yes, I no longer think it's Pollyanna whitewash. And I will have to see how it translates over to my work as a CEO."

Allen smiled. "Thanks. And yeah, I know what you mean. This *is* hard work."

Three o'clock in the morning. Isabel woke up from a dream. She lay still, listening to the random rhythm of the rain hitting the roof. She was dreading tomorrow, the last day of the retreat. They had all been charged with designing a long-term personal leadership project. It had to be a project that she had a passion for and that she was willing to devote significant, ongoing time and energy to accomplish. So far, she had come up with precisely nothing, nada, zilch.

Oh, she could say the foundation where she worked was her leadership project, but she knew that was a cop-out. That was a job, not a quest. Nothing in there was calling her. Then she remembered the dream she had been having just before she woke up. In the dream, she was flying home from the retreat in her car. She looked down at waves crashing against the rocky California coastline. Then she banked left and headed back into civilization. The landscape changed. Below her were burned-out buildings, steel skeletons of what had once been skyscrapers, collapsed bridges, and empty highways, cracked and warped. In the distance, sand was blowing in to cover them all. Isabel looked behind her and saw a bile-green plume of smoke coming from her car-airplane. She knew that this was all her fault, that she had poisoned everything.

Isabel rolled over and pulled her blankets up to her chin. It was going to be a long night. Would this rain never stop?

Emily's voice woke her up. "Isabel, it's getting near breakfast time. Wake up!" Isabel rolled over and glared at her.

"Sweetie, what's the matter?" asked Emily.

"Bad night. Nasty dreams."

Emily swung her legs over and sat on the edge of her bed.

"Tell me."

Isabel just wanted her to go away. She was about to say, "I'd rather not talk about it right now," but she saw how cute and sincere Emily looked. Oh well. Intimacy, right? So she told Emily about her post-apocalyptic vision.

"Sounds awful. Is that some sort of guilt for driving your fancy new Lexus?"

"No guilt with my car. It's an HS hybrid. I get over thirty-five miles per gallon. Many years ago, I was a rabid green activist, almost an Earth First! eco-guerrilla. But I grew out of that phase. No, this was just a bad dream."

The rain was still pouring down outside the event room. Every Unicorn sat in silence, writing in their journals. Isabel faced an empty page. She was supposed to be designing the presentation she had to make to the tribe about her leadership project. All she had was emptiness. She finally gave up trying to figure out what to do and just sat there.

Then a memory came back from her college days. She was sitting in her dorm room, arguing loudly with several other fellow activists about how to protest the university's plan to bulldoze a park to build student housing. She remembered thinking at that time that protesting was stupid; no one cared about what a bunch of students thought. Damn, if only she were older, then she could really make a difference!

What had she become? She used to see herself as a fierce warrior for the earth and for her children. She was a Danger type, and back in those days, she was ready to fight for the earth. But then she grew up and put those childish things away. Had she outgrown her caring about the planet or just let her life get caught up in other, more urgent but less important things? Immediately she heard a voice in her head saying, *Oh, grow up! You're too old to make any difference now.*

This empty shell who walked around calling herself Isabel wasn't really her! Here she was, older, smarter, and a lot more powerful. Maybe this was the time she had been waiting for. She started to write.

When it was her turn to declare her leadership project to the tribe, she took one last look at her journal, then shut it and put it on her chair. She walked up to the front of the room.

"This life is all we have. This planet is all we have. If we want life to survive, we must find a way to sustain all life on this tiny ball spinning through the universe. Big business has been seen as the enemy of sustainability, putting short-term profits over long-term benefits to the environment. Sometimes it lives up to that image, and sometimes it tries to lessen its harmful impact.

"I intend to support sustainability, first in my own nonprofit company, and then in the world."

She had no idea how to proceed. But she felt stronger than she had in a long time. After the group session was over. Stella came over to her and handed her a sheet of paper.

"Call this guy after the retreat is over. I think your project will dovetail nicely with what he is doing."

Isabel looked down on the slip of paper. On it was a long international phone number and the name Ted van der Put.

Key Leadership Concepts in Retreat Three

Particles: All of the separate objects that make up the universe we call particles. Particles are the things we keep bumping into. The most important particles, for a leader, are the people whom he or she leads. Our culture obsesses about managing particles.

Space: Particles move around in space. There is vastly more space than there are particles. Space has a complexion, an energy, and a presence all its own, distinct from the presence of all the particles bouncing around inside it. Our language has very few words to describe the nature of this ubiquitous element called space. Great leaders have an innate ability to sense the space that surrounds and encloses the particles. They find ways to focus on and transform the space between the particles.

The Level Three is the emotional field in the space. Every thought, every change in facial muscles, every gesture, action, and word we say, has an impact on the Level Three.

Arcs: Great leaders have an innate understanding of timing. The right timing is a pace that is both perfectly aligned with the needs of the space and matched to the leaders' own rhythms.

Arcus prolongus: Continuing an activity beyond its natural time span.

Arcus interruptus: Cutting an activity short before its natural time span.

Don't sacrifice the needs of the group to address the needs of one problem individual. Keeping one's attention as a leader on the space of the room, and staying attuned to what that space needs, is hard to get used to for professional helpers in any capacity—managers, teachers, parents, or therapists. They are drawn to doing intense one-on-one work like moths to the flame. Doing this can alienate, bore, or irritate the group as a whole and can subvert the needs of the Leader's Stake. Pay attention first to the space and only secondarily to the individual, or you might go down burning.

Chapter Seven

Journey into Alliance

The moment one definitely commits oneself, then providence moves too. All sorts of things occur to help one that would never otherwise have occurred. A whole stream of events issues from the decision, raising in one's favor all manner of unforeseen incidents, meetings, and material assistance which no man could have dreamed would have come his way. Whatever you can do or dream you can, begin it. Boldness has genius, power, and magic in it. Begin it now.

Attributed to Goethe

Isabel checked the clock for the fifth time and then did the math. Okay, it was morning in Europe. She settled her yellow pad on her lap and began to dial.

"Hello, Mr. van der Put, this is Isabel Lopez. I know you said in your email that this would be a good time to talk, but I just want to make sure it works for you."

His voice had a European accent that Isabel couldn't quite pin down.

"Stella Mancusi is one of your leaders, right?"

"Uh, yes."

"She was a leader in my tribe when I went through Leadership. Great woman—I totally loved her. Sure, let's talk; I have an hour at least. So, why did she tell you to call me?"

Isabel sighed. "Okay, this is going to sound a little strange coming from me, so you have to trust me that I am not a hippie chick living on an organic farm in Oregon when I say what I am about to say. I am the CEO of one of the larger nonprofit service agencies in the United States. We serve the indigent, disabled members of our population.

"That said, my Leadership Quest is to bring the concepts of sustainability and ecological awareness to nonprofit and for-profit corporate leaders. Insanely idealistic, I know, and I have a hard time even saying those words."

Ted laughed. "Just finished your third retreat, right?"

"Yes."

"Figures. Doesn't Leadership completely mess with our pragmatic corporate minds? I know what you are going through. Want to hear my story?"

"Sure."

"I spent twenty-five years climbing up the corporate ladder. But on that beautiful, traditional, well-acknowledged career path, I realized that as I became more and more successful, I felt more and more that something was missing.

"Then my wife inspired me to try Leadership. During that damn third retreat, I was sitting on a mountain looking over the sea. And I realized that I was having access to some deep source of gratitude and love inside me, a source that had been difficult to access before. Looking at the beautiful world before me, I deeply felt that it was time for me to pay back all that I owed to this beautiful, bountiful earth of ours.

"I realized that the whole issue of climate change is not something that can be left to politicians or nongovernmental organizations to fix. I saw that multinational corporations, with all their reach, talent, management skills, creativity, and technology, should and could play their part in shifting the paradigm toward sustainability. So I decided that, with my background in working at many levels of a multinational, I could be instrumental in helping that unfold at a boardroom level.

"I wasn't sure how, but I really felt that multinational corporations should lead the way in demonstrating how to move from serving shareholders to serving all their stakeholders, including the earth itself. That Stake never changes, even though these days I am focusing more on educating the next group of CEOs and a little less on changing the minds of the ones already in power.

"So that moment on the mountain was the genesis of my leadership project. No, Isabel, your ideas don't sound too idealistic to me."

When she hung up after the call, Isabel realized that she had quite a challenge ahead of her. She looked at the full page of notes she had taken. Then she turned the page and wrote, *Isabel, what about you?*

She had to deal with the beam in her own eye before she went out to lecture about the mote in the eyes of all those other CEOs. This wasn't about just putting up some recycling bins. She had to start by transforming the culture of her own company. Sustainability and ecological awareness had to become central to every decision. This would mean educating from the top down, starting with her board. She needed to get them solidly behind her before she started in on her managers. Suddenly, a dream she had had in Leadership came back to her. Yes, Grandmother Luisa had been right when she said, "Step lightly, Isabel!"

It was time to bring up sustainability with her board. Isabel wondered if she could persuade them to bring Ted van der Put to help her train them.

Violet reached across the table and took Isabel's hands in her own.

"Isabel, it's time for 'The Talk.'"

Isabel flinched, and Violet felt it. "Don't worry, honey, this isn't a 'I have my bedroom set in the back of the pickup, and where should I put it?' kind of talk. But we've been dating for six months, and I just want to know where we are going with this relationship. Do you want us to go deeper or just stay where we are with it?"

Isabel looked at her young yet wise lover. Isabel hated these talks. Her initial reaction was usually close to rage. She wanted to snap at her, "Just leave it alone!" But she had to self-manage that reaction with an iron hand. If she wasn't careful, she would drive away the one woman she really wanted to be with. Instead, she sighed.

"Is it that bad?" Violet asked.

"It's just a hard time right now with my mother, and . . ." Then she just trailed off into silence, which wasn't like her.

Finally, Violet replied, "Yes, I know. And are you going to go it alone, like the good, stoic girl you are, never asking for help and rarely even talking about it? That's part of what I'm talking about. Are you going to let me in or not?"

Here it was, right in Isabel's face. She was unwilling to ask for help. She always needed to be in control. She constantly judged herself, convincing herself that she didn't deserve other people's help, and that, in any case, they would probably mess it up or let her down. And she felt the loneliness that came from all that.

All of the issues that had made Leadership such a struggle for her were showing up again with Violet. She took her hands from Violet's and said, "If you could give me a minute, there's something inside me that I need to work out."

Violet smiled. "No problem. I'll be right here."

Isabel thought, *So, instead of beating myself up or blaming Violet, what else can I do? Well, what is my Stake in this moment? What do I want with this relationship? I like Violet a lot and am very attracted to her. And she is one of the few women I know who can get in my face, like she is doing right now, and not attack me or collapse when I react. She's not intimidated at all by me. And she is adorable! I'm scared because I like her a lot. Almost too much. I don't want to be hurt the way my ex Francine hurt me. My Stake, I guess, is 'Leaders and lovers step toward fear, not away from it.' God, right now I want to throw up.*

Then Isabel intentionally softened her focus. She stopped obsessing about her fear, and even stopped focusing so intently on Violet. She took a deep breath and then opened up to the energy around her. She could feel the whole room waiting. It was hushed, like a theater just before the curtain rises. This was her moment to take action and to change the story of her life. She looked up at Violet.

"Okay, so what do *you* want?"

Violet said, "I want to be a bigger part of your life. I want to feel like I am important to you. I want you to dare to need me."

Isabel could feel something start to melt. It was time to stop protecting herself from hurt. She loved Violet. And, sure, she might get hurt someday. But love was worth the price.

Isabel fought back a tear. She swallowed and then said, "Okay, a little step. She probably won't know which one of us is her daughter, but can you come with me this afternoon to see my mother?"

Chapter Eight

Creating from Everything

In the course of history, there comes a time when humanity is called to shift to a new level of consciousness, to reach a higher moral ground. A time when we have to shed our fear and give hope to each other. That time is now.

Wangari Maathai

Allen was composing his monthly bulletin to parish leaders:

In the Book of Revelations, it is written that the dragon of evil is to be cast down into the fiery pit for a thousand years. Then it will be let out for a while to spread chaos and deceive nations. Once more it is to be cast down into the pit, for another thousand years.

That was written some two thousand years ago. Some of you might be wondering if the dragon has been unleashed again. Especially now that Bishop Williams has been hospitalized with a mild stroke, attendance is lower than it was at this time last year, and money is very tight.

It is in times like these that our faith gets tested. However, there are tiny miracles every week that can help us restore it. Let me share three of those stories that were sent to me this month from parishes throughout the diocese.

A truck came rumbling past, disrupting his flow. To hell with it! Allen stood up, stretched, and walked away from the computer. He was sick of this job. He knew he was going to finish the newsletter, and it might bring a little inspiration to the leaders in the parishes who actually read it. But he was an Anglican minister, not a journalist. This wasn't the kind of work that touched and inspired him. He wanted a flock again.

After his "indiscretion" with a parishioner, he had been taken out of direct ministry. Now he was stuck in an office job, responsible for being a liaison between sixteen parishes, as well as representing his district to the diocese. He wasn't even sure exactly what his job entailed, since the duties seemed to change with the weather. On top of that, his bishop was currently in the hospital, and the provisional bishop was continually critical and a stickler for orthodoxy. Allen felt judged every minute he had to be in the same room with that gentleman, and he struggled to avoid him like the plague. Allen missed his real bishop's guidance and needed it badly right now. Every day, he seemed to make a new mistake at work, none of which escaped the provisional bishop's notice. He dreaded those inevitable, irritated phone calls.

These days, his home life was almost worse. His wife had gotten the house in the divorce settlement. Before the divorce, home had been a friendly refuge, a gathering place for the members of their congregation. Now, it was a quiet, lonely, cold, and tiny apartment. On the weekends when Kimberly, his daughter, visited, it was filled with her hyperkinetic energy. Their schedule was action packed with miniature golf, hikes in the park, late forays to the all-night ice cream parlor, and craft projects or jigsaw puzzles that covered every surface of the apartment. But now Kimberly was at camp for the summer, and Allan dreaded going home every night to the cold, empty space.

His relationship with God was also shifting, and not in a direction he liked. Where once he had felt the Lord's guidance and firm direction showing him the way, now there was silence. He could feel the Lord's presence, but only as a stillness, not as a higher advisor. His life was now his to figure out, and Allen missed this connection. Yet another of his companions distancing himself. Or maybe it was Allen himself who was creating the distance. He didn't know, but it felt sad.

And tomorrow he was going to the last leadership retreat! Knowing that Leadership was ending loomed over him like a storm cloud. He really wanted just to stay on retreat forever and not have to go back to the uncertainty and dissatisfaction that would undoubtedly face him when he returned. His loneliness was killing him, and he longed to see a room filled with friendly faces again. He missed the tribe, the intimacy, and the learning. He especially wasn't looking forward to saying good-bye for the last time. This was their last retreat, and that meant yet more changes, more losses.

Eventual separation is the price of love, he thought. *Maybe I should write about that in my bulletin. Not so uplifting, though. It would never get past my provisional bishop.* Reluctantly, he walked back over to his desk and began typing.

As **Allen** drove up the winding road to the retreat center, he wondered what would face him. One tribe member had officially dropped out of the program after the last retreat, claiming too many family responsibilities. Allen wasn't buying it. Robert had always stayed closed and one step removed from the rest of the tribe. Nobody seemed to know him that well. It was no surprise that he wanted to avoid whatever this last gathering would bring up. Allen wouldn't miss him.

The closer he got, the more slowly he drove. Finally, he stopped at a small diner just before the turnoff to the retreat center. Nursing a cup of bitter coffee, he sat there, feeling the mess of emotions inside him. This really sucked!

As soon as he drove up to the retreat center and got out of his car, the clouds around him began to dissipate. Phil came running over and gave him a bear hug.

"Allen, you dog. It's great to see you. Want to room with me for this retreat?"

He was wanted. Something inside Allen that had been holding on tightly for weeks relaxed.

"I'd love that. What cabin do we have?"

Just then, two arms grabbed him from behind and he heard Emily's voice.

"Allen, thank goodness you're here. It's about time. I was getting worried you weren't going to come. Unpack later. You cut that one pretty close. Hurry up—we're starting the opening session in five minutes."

He was back with his tribe.

The three of them were just sitting down as the bell rang to begin the first session. Looking around at the circle, Allen saw that every chair was filled. He remembered how some of them had arrived late to the first meeting of the first leadership retreat, and how disconcerting that had been. Today everyone was showing up on time—leaders taking responsibility for their impact.

Stella laughed. "Nice job, Unicorns—all here on time. Glad you just made it, Allen. This is going to be good. Leadership is happening from the very beginning. I love that. Responsibility is being taken. Looks like we're really ready to launch this retreat."

Zeke took off his sheepskin jacket. "Yep. Let's launch. Now, in the last retreat, we worked with the emptiness of the space. We explored the emptiness inside us, and we felt into the wide-open, infinite space that is all around us in every moment. We sensed that space, and then we noticed our impact on it. We cleared ourselves out with meditation exercises and visualizations where we drained away all distracting thoughts, feelings, and opinions. From that inner emptiness, we learned how to create from nothing.

"In this retreat, we'll be exploring the space and noticing how full it is all the time. We will be dancing in the chaos that is always in the space. We will be learning how to move through chaos and even embrace it, rather than being overwhelmed by it."

Stella laughed. "I just saw the look on some of your faces. Yes, I know. Embrace chaos? Now we really *are* going off the deep end. Usually we dread chaos. How often do we rub our hands in glee when the space gets messy and chaotic? After this retreat, you will know that chaos is your best friend. How can we dive in with gusto to dance with it and to find the patterns and pathways in it? How can we make choices about what to pay attention to in the space, and what to let go of? And, perhaps most importantly, how can we take responsibility for the space and lead in it?"

Zeke said, "Yes, this is the retreat in which we start to develop our facility with multiple screens. Ah, more jargon! Well, let me tell you what I mean by that.

"Imagine you are a TV director in a news or sports booth. You have dozens of small screens of live action happening in front of you, and you have the main broadcast screen that holds the central focus. You need to be aware all the time of what is on every one of the other screens, so that you can throw the switch at any moment and bring any one of the alternative screens up on the central-focus screen."

"That's what it's like as a leader in every moment," Stella added. "You have a Leader's Stake, the lens you're looking through all the time, looking at all the screens going on around you, and you keep choosing the screen that will best serve that Stake in any given moment."

"Okay," said Zeke. "So for this exercise, my Stake is 'Leaders lead from everything.' Right now, my main broadcast screen is actually focused on me, talking about multiple screens. At the same time, I'm aware of a screen that is showing me what is going on with the Level Three of the room, which is alert and a little confused.

Also, there's a screen that shows Stella; where she's going and what she's doing. Right now, for example, she's waiting to see if she has anything to add to what I am saying.

"Then there's a screen for each one of you in my field of awareness. For example, I'm aware that Isabel is getting restless. There's a screen for my own body, how I feel and my internal state, which right now is pain-free and energized. Unfortunately, there's a saboteur screen that's telling me I'm not getting the job done, but I have a lot of skill at minimizing that one. There's a screen for holding time: the time line and an awareness of what is coming next. And there's even a screen for logistics that pays attention to when we need to eat next or take a break.

"I'm holding all these screens in my awareness simultaneously, all the time. I can move any one of them up to the central screen at any point. I'll do so whenever I feel that focusing on another screen is going to serve the Stake and the learning in the room more powerfully than the one I'm currently focused on. This ability to hold multiple screens is crucial to being able to dance with all that is going on in the space in any given moment.

"You need to get skilled at being able to do this easily, almost unconsciously. And you need to learn how to let go of your natural concern about getting it right. Just know that you will often make mistakes about what should be on that main screen. That doesn't actually matter, because as long as you're looking through the lens of your Stake, if one screen fails to serve it, you just choose another screen to put up."

Then Stella chimed in, "The main problem that most of us have is that we get focused on a single screen. We invest all our chips in that one picture. So when other stuff starts to happen, it knocks us off stride. It distracts us. So we hunker down and work with that one screen even harder. We begin to ignore the Level Three. The more we do that, the faster we fly off the model and head toward authoritarian leadership.

"For instance, if I were convinced that the content about multiple screens was essential, I could lecture about it for an hour and end up losing the attention of the whole room. All my other screens would go dark except the one with the lecture notes on it."

"And then you'd have to call the cable guy," Zeke added.

After the laughter ebbed, Stella went on.

"At other times, what we're following on this main screen starts to wander in a direction that isn't related to our Stake. When that happens, we can get so fascinated by it, or so focused on that irrelevant screen and what is going on, that we forget our Stake and fly off the model. For example, if I were feeling very hungry right now, I might start to hurry through this material to get something to eat sooner.

"Either way, we're off the model and stuck in our reactions. But when we're aware of the multiple screens, we can stay on the model and stay on task, focused on our Stake. We can stay flexible and agile with the space, and with every screen we're viewing."

Zeke said, "Also, in this retreat, we'll expand our ability to move quickly from one emotional truth, mood, or quality to an entirely different one, sometimes in a heartbeat. And that means shifting the energy of the whole room, not just your own.

"Why do we need to know how to shift the room like that? It's always for the sake of the Stake. In this retreat, you will learn to create from everything that is happening inside you and all around you in any given moment."

Stella said, "Now we're going to switch the focus completely, away from two leaders pontificating in the front of the room and over to you leading yourselves. This is your tribe meeting time. Use the next two hours however you want to as a tribe. We'll be in the back of the room, and we may or may not interrupt. Right now, two leaders need to come up and lead this meeting."

And with that, she and Zeke walked to the back of the room, leaving their own two chairs empty.

Allen was amazed to find himself standing up and moving to the front of the room. He had thought he would just sit back and watch, but something inside him pushed him up on his feet and out to the front.

He looked over at his co-leader as he sat down. This was the first time he had ever led with Emily. She smiled at him and said, "Oh boy. Here we go."

Allen looked out at the circle of familiar faces looking expectantly at him. He thought, *This is just like being in the pulpit; the congregation is looking to me, and I have no idea what to say.*

Much to Allen's relief, Emily spoke first. He breathed a huge sigh of relief. Unlike being in the pulpit, here he wasn't alone. Now he had a co-leader!

"Okay, boys and girls, so here we are in our last retreat together in this program, although I hope it isn't the last time we get together as a tribe. So, what do we want to do with this meeting?"

Allen had a vision of the possible chaos of everyone tossing out ideas for what to do. Turning the agenda over to the group didn't fit with his idea of what a leader does. He saw tears running down Olivia's face. He decided to step in and take charge, hoping his leader would trust him and follow him.

"Olivia, I see you are crying. Tell us what is going on."

It took Olivia a minute to reply, which seemed like forever to Allen. Then she said, "I just feel so sad that it's all ending. I feel so close to all of you, and it's almost over." She started crying again.

Allen didn't know what to do with Olivia's tears. Emily walked across the room and put her arms around her. Olivia stopped sobbing, but tears were still running down her face. She turned to Emily and said, "I'm sorry."

"It's okay," said Emily.

At that moment, Zeke stood up and said loudly, "Stop!" Everyone froze. Then he said, "Emily, all you really did was smooth over the space. Olivia is speaking for something that is in this space. By reassuring her, patting her down, and making things nice, you didn't get to discover what she was speaking for.

"There's pain in this room, and it's not just Olivia's. This is your last retreat, and there's a ton of strong emotions about it. Don't shut them down. Open them up, and let's find out what's here. Remember what I told you in the last retreat: serve the Stake and the space, and don't just focus on the individuals. Now continue." As he sat back down, Emily left Olivia and walked back to her seat in the front of the room.

"Okay, so there's a bunch of stuff floating around." Then she gestured with open arms. "Come on, let's have it all."

Three people started to speak at the same time.

Allen said, "Great, we'll have time to hear from everyone. Let's start with you, Phil."

Phil said, "Okay, I'm pissed at Robert for copping out on us!"

Isabel said, "No kidding!"

Phil said, "But I don't want someone who isn't even here to mess up my retreat—well, I mean, *our* retreat. . . "

Two hours later, during the debriefing that followed the tribe meeting, Zeke talked some more about what had happened with Emily and Allen's leadership.

"By now, we're all able to notice and read our impact on the Level Three. So now we're ready to begin looking at how to take responsibility for it. Look at our model of Co-Active Leadership. At the bottom is an arrow with the word *Act* underneath it. Over to the left are two bubbles side by side: *Full Permission* and *Responsibility for Impact*.

"These two may seem a bit paradoxical. With Full Permission, the action takes place authentically, with no holding back or editing. With Responsibility for Impact, you are aware of the impact you are actually having and the impact that you intended to have, and you are completely responsible for it.

"In the third retreat, we asked you to silence the critics and have a lot of impact all over the place so that you could notice the impact of your Full Permission on the space, without trying to be 'nice' or 'brilliant' or 'successful.' Remember the first ten minutes of the web exercise? Lots of Full Permission and a wonderful, ineffectual mess. You began to notice those ripples and how they impact the Level Three. Now it's time to work on being responsible for that impact."

The Co-Active® Leadership Model

Stella jumped in. "First of all, let's talk about responsibility. For most people, that word carries such a burden of being in charge of things. It implies having to do those things right and well. It also often means editing out the extremes of our range of emotions and expressions. We often feel compelled to filter out our emotions and our wilder ideas so that we operate in an 'acceptable' manner in our presentation or action.

"Of course, that isn't what *we* mean by *responsibility* in this context. The first way I want to talk about responsibility is as our ability to respond, our 'respond-ability.' Now that you can read your impact on the space, it's time to learn how to respond instantly to that impact, and then how to work with the next urge that emerges."

Zeke agreed. "Right, so Responsibility for Impact has a lot to do with how agile you are at responding to the impact you create in the space. It also has to do with your intention, your ability to craft the impact that you want to create in the space, and then to create impact, moment by moment, again and again, dancing within a wide range of actions and impacts that you can have on the space."

Stella said, "Rather than dancing, more often than not, we run around fixing the actions that we just did. We check out how our actions 'landed' with the people in the room. If what we just did failed and we didn't get the results we intended, then we try to manage our own negative reactions. We say, 'Damn these people, why don't they get it?' Then we might take all sorts of roads, all leading away from Co-Active Leadership."

"Right," added Zeke. "We might take the easy road, where we adjust what we do or try to fix the mess we made so that no one stays offended and things remain comfortable and safe, even if that means we have to abandon our point or our Stake. Or we take the harder road, where we start to judge, berate, and push against the people we are trying to lead because they are not going the way we want them to go. This might seem to serve the Stake, but actually, attacking or disempowering people never serves your Stake."

Stella liked Zeke's metaphor. "Or we might abandon all those country roads and jump over to the freeway. If what we did just bombed, we shut down all this reactive feedback and unproductive conversation in the name of efficiency. We just go on to the next agenda item. This makes it clear to our audience that any experiences that are not positive are useless and should be ignored by all of us."

Zeke carried right on. "None of these paths represents responsible leadership in our model. In this retreat, we're asking you to take responsibility in a completely different way. You can't fall back into overly nice and compliant leadership, and you can't barrel into authoritarian leadership. We want you to discover what it means to lead by responding fully to the space, to the people you lead, and by holding on to your Stake. We'll be doing lots of exercises and giving you lots of experiences to land this in your bones, so that you'll learn to replace your automatic reactions with respond-ability for every action and for every impact that you have on the space.

"Leading from everything, and taking responsibility for the space, doesn't end in the meeting room or with the work group. A leader interacts with regulating agencies, community groups, unions, reporters, sometimes even foreign governments. Leading means being fully aware of the total environment in which you lead. That means holding in your awareness the needs and positions of every Stakeholder and taking responsibility for impacting that entire, vast ecosystem in which you operate, in a way that advances your Stake and stays true to your values and Life Purpose."

That afternoon, they did a physical exercise called Individual and Paired *Rondori*. It permanently changed Allen's view of himself. The exercise started with the tribe standing in a large circle. In the first part of the exercise, one tribe member stood in the middle of the circle while the rest of the tribe, at random intervals, walked straight toward him and continued across to the opposite side of the circle. Sometimes, two or three people started toward the middle at the same time. The job of the person in the middle was simply not to be touched by anyone. For Allen, being in the middle was like slow-motion bumper cars. He could easily avoid the people he could see, but he kept getting surprised by people coming from behind him.

When it was Olivia's turn to be in the middle, Allen watched her dance through the mob of people who came at her, turning the exercise into a ballet. The way she could anticipate the moving bodies and then become a mist that floated untouched between them was quite beautiful. He saw how she moved into the empty spaces, rather than always trying to avoid the bodies.

Then Zeke and Stella added more chaos and complexity to the event. In Paired *Rondori*, two people stood in the center. As in the first exercise, the pair in the middle had to avoid being bumped as people walked across the circle. If either one of the pair was touched, then the pair's turn in the middle was over. Also, the leaders played a piece of music in which bells rang at random moments. Whenever a bell rang, the pair had three seconds to make some sort of physical contact with each other, or their turn ended right there.

When each member of the pair in the middle was operating individually, Allen saw couple after couple dance elegantly around the oncoming bodies. But once that bell rang and they started trying to connect, they would get so focused on making contact with each other that they would lose their connection with everyone else in their space, and one or the other of them would get bumped by someone else. He figured the same thing was going to happen to him, which was too bad, because he was paired with Olivia, the tiny dancer, and they would be the last pair. She deserved a better partner than he, Mr. Bull in a China Shop!

But as they stood together in the center of the room, waiting for the music to start, something amazing happened to his awareness. His focus softened. Time seemed to slow down, and he sensed an imaginary silver thread connecting him with Olivia. As other bodies started coming toward him, he stepped effortlessly into the space around them, simultaneously aware of everyone moving everywhere in the room. No matter where he was in the room, he felt himself always in contact with one end of the silver thread that connected him with Olivia.

At first, they easily made connection when the bell rang, sometimes touching fingertips around other people's moving bodies. Then something even more magical began happening. They began to anticipate the random bells. They would be across the room from each other, gliding around bodies, and then simultaneously start moving toward the center and bump hips just as the next bell rang.

Finally, the leaders had to stop the game, because it was clear that no one could interfere with their dance. They were completely in sync. As the music stopped, Allen and Olivia hugged. Then the rest of the tribe mobbed them. Everyone was cheering. Allen had never felt so graceful in his whole life.

The **next** day, the atmosphere at breakfast was electric. No one knew what was up, but everyone had ideas. There was going to be some kind of secret, all-day activity that had been hinted at in Retreat Three. The gossip in the tribe was that they would be doing something off-site, but no one knew what that something might be. They were all in their seats in the meeting room ahead of schedule.

Stella began to speak: "Leaders serve. What are people talking about when they talk about servant leadership? We believe that we are always in service to the ongoing dream of life, the unfolding, life-affirming story of the universe. So, at a meta-level, all leadership is in service to that story and in service to the evolution of human consciousness.

"People often get confused when their leadership is in service to their own ego, or to a specific group of egos, or even in service to some company mission. These are all shaky things for your leadership to be in service to. They're ephemeral and mundane. You need to have a really big picture and set a Stake that serves the greatest good.

"Now, there's another aspect of servant leadership that has to do more with the space that we are leading in. We serve the space. How do we do that? It's right there on the model. You know that we *Act* with *Full Permission* and *Responsibility for Impact*, based on the *Urge* and always serving the *Leader's Stake*. Then we *Stay* with our impact. We notice what our impact was on the space or on the Level Three of the space. Then we ask ourselves, 'What's needed next?' This question of service is 'What is the next urge that will produce the next action?' When we *Stay* and check into that question, we are leaders in service, serving the space around us and serving our Stake."

Then Zeke chimed in, "Leaders serve those they lead. So your mission today is to serve. You will be in groups of four. Each group will go to a different town. Your job is to find an organization, a company, or a group in that town for which you can provide service and leadership. All four of you in a group must stay together, work together, and spend at least two hours in that act of service.

"There are maps along the walls that show the town assigned to each group. That's where you'll look for the people you are going to serve. Each group has a car and driver, so find the map with your name on it and get together. You have ten minutes to do some planning, and then you need to be on the road. You need to be back here in your seats by four o'clock this afternoon. Those are all the instructions we are giving you. Have fun, lead, and serve well." Then Stella and Zeke stood up and left the room.

Chaos reigned as everyone started talking at once while running along the walls, looking for their groups. Allen finally found the map with his name on it. He was glad to see that he was with three of his favorite tribe members: Isabel, Emily, and Phil. Emily took over: "Okay, grab your sunscreen, your journals, and anything else you think you might need. We'll be in the green Prius. Let's get going. We can plan in the car."

As Allen was walking back to his room, he thought, *Where did meek little Emily go?*

They weren't two minutes into the journey before Isabel and Phil were arguing over strategy. Phil was suggesting that they stop at the library and ask for help, while Isabel was insisting all they needed to do was call the local volunteer bureau.

From the driver's seat, Emily said, "Stop it, you two. This feels crappy. I don't know why, but it does."

Allen knew why it felt crappy. "Thanks, Emily, I felt that way, too. So, have we learned anything in this program? We are jumping into all this strategizing and planning without having alignment or a Stake. It looks like this leadership program just went flying out the window. Oopsie-poopsie!"

All four of them laughed at themselves. Then a much more interesting debate began, about what they all could align around as a Stake. The other three were quite surprised when Phil finally came up with one they all loved: "Staying open to synchronicity guides us to the highest service."

Allen gave a contented sigh. "Ah, that feels right, doesn't it?" Everyone agreed.

They were just entering Nester Valley, the town circled on their map, when Emily said, "Look over there. I guess Mr. Synchronicity was listening."

The sign read **Streamwood Elder Community: Committed to Serving Seniors**. To a chorus of "Okay" and "Let's do it," Emily turned her car into the curving entry drive.

Their offer to spend a day volunteering was welcomed by Mary, the coordinator at the main house. Each of them was assigned to assist in a different live-in facility. When Mary heard that Allen could play the piano and sing, she sent him off to the recreational room in the assisted-living center.

As he walked into the room, the smell of Pine-Sol, with a hint of urine underneath, took him aback for a moment. But he'd been in plenty of senior-care facilities in his work, and this one was cleaner and better organized than most. A group of residents was watching a cooking show on television, and four others were playing cards in the corner. No one looked over at him as he entered.

Well, he thought, *this is certainly a leadership opportunity.* He spotted the baby-grand piano off to the side. He walked over to it and sat down. He was pleased to find that all the keys appeared to be in working order, and even more pleased to discover that the instrument was more or less in tune. He thought about his interpretation of the group's Stake: "Today we trust the universe to guide us to where we need to be, and to show us how we are meant to change people's lives. Well, here I am. Let's see what happens."

He began to play an old Beatles song, "In My Life," singing it softly to himself. At the end of the song, he looked up and saw that one of the card players had abandoned her card game to sit behind him. Smiling, the woman asked, "Do you know 'September Song'? I used to love listening to Willie Nelson singing it."

Allen started playing a few bars and said, "Sure. Do you want to join me?"

She protested that she couldn't sing but stood next to him and started out softly: "Oh, it's a long, long time . . ." Soon she was singing along.

They sang a couple of songs together, with him mostly singing and her mostly humming. But then something began to feel wrong. He looked around the room and saw that hardly anything had changed in the space of the recreation room. The TV was still playing some reality show. The card game was going on, unaffected by his attempt at leadership. Something wasn't right about this.

He remembered Zeke saying they were supposed to stay together. He felt incomplete doing this alone. He thought about how, throughout the leadership program, there were always at least two leaders in the front of the room. Then he thought about himself, the lone wolf typing away on parish bulletins, solitary and miserable. There had to be a better way for him to serve. So he excused himself from the singing and went in search of a fellow Unicorn.

He ran into Emily, who was mopping a floor and chatting with one of the community's coworkers.

He asked, "Excuse me, but would you mind if I kind of borrowed Emily? I need her to help me with my project."

The woman laughed. "Hell, that's okay, take her away. I loved the company, but I have mopped plenty of floors in my time. Go help your friend, girl."

As Emily and Allen headed back to the rec room, Emily asked, "So what's up?"

Allen said, "I started playing the piano, and one lady joined me, but somehow it didn't really feel like I was making much of an impact."

"I know. I mean, I was having a great conversation with Ethel back there, but it was more like just helping out, not like leading."

Allen stopped walking and faced Emily. "Okay, so what is our Stake for the rec room?"

"Well, it sounds like it's something to do with music and bringing people together."

Allen agreed. "Yes, how about 'Music unites souls and creates community'? Up for it?"

Emily smiled. "Perfect. Let's rock and roll!"

Allen sat down at the piano and, reacting to Emily's comment, broke into a spirited piano intro to "Rock and Roll Music." Emily picked it up and belted it out.

"Just let me hear some of that rock and roll music . . ."

One of the card players, in a wheelchair, tossed in his hand, pushed himself over to the people watching the TV, and asked them to turn it down. Instead they muted it completely, and most of them came over to listen to the music. By the time Allen and Emily got to the last stanza, the rest of the card players had joined their growing audience. Then someone called out, "Do you know 'Love Me Tender'?"

Allen turned around to his growing audience. "We sure do, but we'll only play it if you all sing along. You can hum along when you don't remember the words. Deal?" Three or four people nodded, so he started playing.

Within ten minutes, all but a couple of people were sitting around the piano, singing and suggesting new songs, most of which Allen and Emily could at least fake their way through. People even started coming down the hall to see what was going on. And when Emily got on the piano and did a version of "Makin' Whoopee," the laughter and applause at the end of that number was riotous. Allen looked up at Emily and whispered, "Sure you aren't a Sex type?"

Emily laughed and quoted Zeke: "We are all these things and much, much more!"

A frail voice yelled out, "How about 'Blue Suede Shoes'?" From then on, they were all singing, laughing, teasing each other, forgetting words, making them up, and having a ball. Allen and Emily were surprised, and even a little disappointed, to hear Isabel at the door, saying, "Okay, troops, time to go back."

Driving back to the retreat center, they all shared their experiences. Isabel had spent most of the time talking with an elderly Mexican American man, who had been delighted to be speaking Spanish and had regaled her with many stories of his life working the oil fields. Phil had done a little acting workshop with four women and had been quite touched by one of them, who was rather delusional. She had decided that he was her husband and had gone on to reenact their wedding ceremony. There were tears in his eyes as he told his story. As Emily and Allen tried to describe their own experience, they all kept breaking into song as they drove.

Back at the retreat, sitting together in the meeting room, all four of them were intrigued to hear the other groups report. One group had failed to find anyone to serve, another had ended up arguing more than serving, and another had had a magical adventure like theirs. For the more successful groups, the two common factors were, first, having had an initial discussion to agree on their Stake, and then having been aligned throughout the day around their group's Stake. The most common mistake had been doing what Allen's group had done at the beginning, with everyone splitting up and going in different directions.

Commenting about Allen's decision to go get help, Zeke said, "The old paradigm of leadership is the lonely hero going off into the wilderness and making things happen. It is time to retire that myth. We all need each other, and there were probably many ways the rest of you could have supported each other in leading while you were serving, not just before and after the experience."

Allen replied, "Yes, it was hard to ask for help at first. But two leaders were always much more powerful than one. We set our group Stake driving along in the car together. I learned that the wording for our Stake didn't come from one leader. It arose naturally out of the discussion. Then one person caught exactly the right phrase and we all knew that was the one. The same thing happened when Emily and I set a Stake for music in the rec room. By leaning in together, we found that the perfect words just arose."

Olivia's group had been spectacularly unsuccessful. She had a question for the leaders: "Okay, so, Zeke, Stella, what are we supposed to do? We got a flat tire. We couldn't agree on how to find a group to serve. One of us got very carsick. The whole thing just sort of blew apart. Then our time was up. Nothing but a big mess. How do you lead from that?"

Stella smiled. "Lots of chaos, right?" Olivia nodded.

Stella said, "We told you that the Stake for this retreat is 'Create from everything.' Well, another way of saying that could be 'Create from chaos.' The way we humans normally relate to chaos is to be frightened of it. We try to fix it and make it go away. Either that or we just give up and let ourselves be overwhelmed and blown away by it. Sounds like giving up was what happened in your group.

"Your experience is pretty common. Things do go sideways. The world seems to be moving faster and faster, and the complexity seems to be increasing geometrically. You all reacted to that by fighting it, and that didn't work very well.

"What you need to do when things go wrong is to see the approaching chaos, rub your hands together in glee, and eagerly look forward to diving into the mess and finding your way through it. You need to be able to recover to this beautiful, circular leadership model over and over again as the gale-force winds of the chaos keep blowing you around. You need to find your way back to the Stake and to keep yourselves acting with Full Permission and Responsibility for Impact."

Zeke jumped in. "When I'm sitting in the center of my purpose and I know clearly why I am here in this life at this time, and when I am channeling that purpose through a clear Stake that's keeping me pointed as a leader in this endeavor, there's a peaceful certainty that lives in my center. With that calm center comes the ability to appreciate and respond to whatever is coming my way—in fact, to anticipate the challenges and the speedy particles as they whiz by me and around me, and to know what to pay attention to and what to let go of as I take my next step down the path.

"As I keep responding in this way, I begin to notice patterns starting to form amid the chaos itself. Pathways begin to open up that provide possibilities and choices to this Grounded Self and leader that I am. I start choosing those pathways that are most clearly aligned with my Stake, and I eventually discover that I'm across the sea of chaos, my tribe is intact, and we're that much closer to the outcomes we're seeking.

"Chaos and challenge actually provide us with a gift—the gift of digging deeper and planting that purpose and Stake more firmly in the ground."

Then Stella said, "Of course, Olivia, you can't do that without a compelling Stake. With this firmly planted and grasped Stake, a leader is able to develop all sorts of flexibility, agility, and creativity in the ways in which she can respond to the chaos swirling around her while keeping her attention on what is needed in the space and the urges that emerge from her Stake. So, what Stake might you have been able to align around today, Olivia?"

"Well, I suggested one: 'Leaders who serve do whatever is asked of them from the space.'"

"Okay, if that was your Stake and you had held to it, how might your experience today have been different?"

"Oh, right! I get it now. I didn't need to go all over town looking for people to serve. They were right there in the car with me."

Zeke said, "Ah, excellent!"

A llen snuck away from the retreat center and drove to Overlook Point, the nearest place where he could get cell phone coverage. He wanted to hear his daughter's voice. And he was in luck: she was doing her homework, not out playing soccer or something.

He talked to her about some of his adventures in leadership and listened to her tale of frustration about a "completely stupid" English teacher. He was going to have to get back to the room soon for the next event. But then Kimberly said something that really rocked him.

"Dad, I'm really glad you are at this leadership thing. You sound happier than I've heard you in a long time. You've been pretty glum lately, and not a whole lot of fun to be around. I hope this thing you are doing helps."

He told her he loved her and said good-bye but didn't drive right back to the center. Instead he sat there, watching the fog bank pile up just offshore, threatening to roll inland. His daughter was right. He hadn't been very happy. Now, what was he going to do about it?

I n the afternoon before the last day of the retreat, Zeke and Stella stood before the tribe.

"This retreat is now yours to lead," Stella said. "Our role as leaders officially ends when Zeke and I walk out of this room. From now on, you're all transitioning from being participants in a leadership program to being leaders who are now responsible for *this* leadership program. Zeke and I will also transition from being the leaders responsible for this program to being wise and respected elders whom the new leaders can call upon if they want."

Zeke added, "In our world, this transition is challenging for both the new leaders and the elders. The new leaders are stepping forth and finding their voices and their own unique pathways and quests. They need to stumble forth on their own, making mistakes and learning while they move forward into this fresh new world that they're creating.

"The elders need to let go of the steering wheel and let the leaders drive the bus. While these new drivers steer things all catawampus for a while, the elders need to have great patience, and a profound sense of wisdom and experience that they can share when needed, without grabbing the steering wheel and taking over."

Stella smiled and elbowed Zeke. "As you can imagine, this will be especially tough on old Zeke here, who likes to pontificate at the slightest provocation. So here you go; the steering wheel is now yours, and we will be around and available should you need any wisdom or resources. As hard as it may be for both you and us, we won't be around to direct you or to teach you anymore. Those are your responsibilities now.

"It's up to you to organize the exercises and rituals for the remainder of the program, and it's your program to bring to a close. Your assignment is to lead the final day, to organize the structure of the day, and to create some sort of completion ceremony for the entire leadership program that you've been in for the year."

Then Zeke added, "Do *not* leave early from this retreat, either energetically or emotionally. Carrying out this final assignment may become challenging at times. But remember, the retreat is not over, and in fact this is the most important part of it. So stay, pay attention to arcs and timing, and practice what you have learned this year."

Then Zeke and Stella left the room.

They went to the dining hall, sat down on the couches at the back of the room, and sighed simultaneously, which made them both chuckle as they looked across at each other.

Zeke said, "So, this is the hardest part for me, darlin', this letting go of that warrior-chief role and handing the spear over to them. This is really an ego-free zone, isn't it?"

Stella pondered for a moment and smiled as she thought of how to answer him as an elder instead of as his co-leader, full of brilliant advice. "You know, my grandmother Kiki used to say, 'Raven, sometimes all you really have to do is breathe and trust, and everything will be just fine.' And Kiki is an Elder with a capital *E*. She's always ready with a story or a parable that makes a brilliant point. Only, on first listen, her stories never seem relevant to what I want to know. But as I ponder it while I'm charging through my busy life, it usually grows on me, until I finally get some meaning out of it.

"Then I'll rush back to Kiki and thank her for pointing me in the right direction, and she'll just smile and breathe and say, 'Honey, all I did was tell you a story. You did the rest.' Zeke, I think that for me, being an elder is channeling Kiki. And if and when any of these leaders come to use me as a resource, I think I'll just share a story with them and have them make their own meaning out of it."

Zeke squirmed a bit and said, "But—uh-oh, I think I'm about to go into whining here—I hate this part of the program! I like being the one with the answers. I don't like letting go of being in control and just making blah-blah-blah."

He paused for a moment. Then he smiled. "Okay, so you're brilliant, as always. You just told me the story of Kiki, didn't you? I guess I should stop and listen to it. I, too, will channel Kiki. Actually, I have my own version of her.

"There was this Taoist storyteller I met once, a guy named Larry, who told the coolest stories that had no obvious ending except the one you made up. He would get near the end of his story, and then a twinkle would come into his eye as he left you hanging. That twinkle seemed to say, *You take this, sonny boy. I know that you'll make a wonderful ending here, a magical ending, and give a rich meaning to the whole journey as well.*

"When I first heard him, I was so pissed, because I just wanted him to finish the story already! Of course, that story worked me and worked me, and eventually I found that the story was the journey and the ending didn't really matter. All that mattered was that moment, that brilliant moment, when he stopped the story and left me with the twinkle in his eye.

"You got me, you beautiful elder, you. I'll play. For the rest of the retreat, it's the Kiki and Larry Show."

After Zeke and Stella left the room, there was a long silence as everyone waited for someone else to do something. But, remarkably for the Unicorns, chaos did not ensue this time and there was no battle for control. They gathered in a circle and sat in silence for a while. Then together they decided that the first thing they needed to do was for each of them to share his or her plan for accomplishing their individual Leadership Quests. They decided that two co-leaders would run this debriefing, and Phil and Emily volunteered.

Allen hated this idea. He wasn't getting anywhere with his Quest. As Isabel, sitting next to him, was finishing up her report, his stomach was granny-knotted. He was next.

She was just finishing her story: "And so I convinced them, based on both ethical and financial grounds. My board committed to building our new national headquarters as an energy-efficient monument to sustainability. It will be built with nontoxic materials, it'll have abundant solar panels and double and triple glazing in all windows, and it will use a solar-heated long-term energy-storage system to generate sustainable, low-cost heat and cooling. After talking with Ted, I realized I needed to begin at home to make the world green, and then work outward from there."

Now it was Allen's turn, and he was sweating a little. "Um, my Quest is to bring some perspectives about Matthew Fox's Creation Spirituality to the attention and consideration of ministers under my supervision. It's not going very far right now."

Olivia said, "From what you told me last night, Allen, that's a bit of an understatement. What's the truth about your Quest?"

Damn. Busted!

"Okay. It's actually dead in the water. My provisional bishop told me to stop rabble-rousing and to focus on my assigned jobs."

Then Emily spoke up. "You know, Allen, I'm stuck, too. And I know the two of us are not alone. How many of us have been less than fabulously successful with this Leadership Quest thing?"

There were more than a few sheepish looks in the room.

She went on, "And I'll bet that for some of you there's a temptation to just chuck the whole thing. But here's the deal. If this leadership program is to mean anything, and if the Unicorns are to have any impact on changing the world, then giving up isn't an option."

Phil picked up Emily's lead and took it in a slightly different direction.

"Yes, we all signed up to make a difference, and we've invested a year of our lives in doing that. So, Allen, I want to focus on you as an example for those of us who may be struggling with their Quests right now. Are you with me?"

Allen trusted Phil. "Go for it."

Phil said, "Isabel just told us about how if she wanted to change the world, she needed to begin by changing her own nonprofit first. You were very passionate about this Creation Spirituality stuff. But you couldn't change your church. And in fact you told me you hated your new job. I am guessing you won't be able to change much of anything if you are miserable."

"So, Allen, what do you really want?" Emily asked.

There was a long silence. Allen kept trying out truths inside his head, looking for the one that was the most resonant. Then a voice inside came, loud and clear.

He said it out loud: "I want a congregation again. I am sick of administration. I want a community where I can just do my work and the Lord's work."

He looked around. Everyone was smiling. They heard the conviction in his voice, and they were right behind him. And he also felt a connection with an energy far greater than him, a presence that he had been separated from for such a long time.

Under his breath he prayed, "Not my will, but thine, be done."

Then Phil said, "Sounds like you just found your true Quest."

It was their final time together, the completion ritual for the end of their fourth retreat. After this the group would split up and go their separate ways, some by car, some on the airport bus. Never again would they all be together in the same place with each other and their leaders. Yes, they had set up monthly tribe conference calls, and some of them were already planning a one-year reunion, but everyone knew that some Unicorns would disappear and this special group would never be together again.

Two by two, they spent some moments in silence, just looking at each other. After their year together, Allen could see how much more alive and connected with each member of the Unicorn Tribe he felt. He knew that some of these people would become his good friends, and that a thread of mutual support and friendship linked them all, no matter what happened from here on. He was crying grateful tears as he said a silent good-bye to each of them.

Key Leadership Concepts in Retreat Four

Creating from Everything: Also known as Creating from Chaos. A masterful leader is able to maintain a global focus on every aspect of the people and details of the project that he or she leads. These leaders never lose sight of the large perspective that inspires their Stake yet can, at the same time, focus down on the most minute detail.

Multiple screens: You have many places to place your attention, and you need to be able to be aware of all of them simultaneously. You choose the screen that will most serve your Stake in any given moment. The main problem that most of us have is that we become focused on a single screen. We invest all our chips into that one picture. So when other stuff starts to happen, it knocks us off stride. It distracts us. Leading from everything is the skill to become unencumbered by individual problems or circumstances while addressing them, if necessary, but only if it serves the Leader's Stake.

Responsibility: Our ability to respond, our respond-ability. Responsibility for Impact has a lot to do with how agile you are at responding to the impact that you create in the space. It also has to do with your intention, with your ability to intend and to craft the impact that you want to create in the space.

Think globally: Taking responsibility for the space and leading from everything doesn't end in the meeting room or with the work group. A leader interacts with regulating agencies, community groups, unions, reporters, sometimes even foreign governments. Leading means being fully aware of the total environment in which you lead. This means holding in your awareness the needs and positions of every Stakeholder; taking responsibility for your impact on that whole vast ecosystem in which you operate, and doing so in a way that advances your Stake and stays true to your values and Life Purpose.

Leaders serve: We are always in service to the ongoing dream of life, the unfolding, life-affirming story of the universe. So, at a meta level, all leadership is in service to that story and in service to the evolution of human consciousness.

Legacy: This is the final challenge of every leader. How to hand it on? Legacy is the process of evolving one's role from that of a leader who is responsible for a Stake to that of an elder who is a wise and respected resource, and whom other leaders can call upon. The elders need to let go of the steering wheel and let the leaders drive the bus. Elders need to hold their profound sense of wisdom and experience available when needed, without grabbing the steering wheel and taking over.

Chapter Nine

Going Home

Men make history and not the other way around. In periods where there is no leadership, society stands still. Progress occurs when courageous, skillful leaders seize the opportunity to change things for the better.

Harry Truman

The retreat was over. Now it was time for the two program leaders to do their final debriefing. Zeke and Stella had retreated to the two overstuffed armchairs in the staff room to begin reviewing this retreat, their dance together as leaders, and the whole life of the Unicorn Tribe.

After an hour, they were winding down. Zeke said, "Well, I think we are almost done here. So, Stella, what was the biggest thing you learned about yourself from the Unicorns? What's your takeaway from this experience?"

Stella laughed. "In conclusion, ladies and gentlemen, I would like to say . . . . Just kidding, Zeke. Actually, it's a good question, even if it was a bit coach-like. What am I taking away? Hmm. The last time I led with you—I think it was a couple of years ago—I kind of gave up on myself and let you do your grandstanding thing. I mean, you do it really well, so I just sort of stepped back and held the space and let you do your thing. Not this time! I really wanted to co-lead as radiant Raven, powerful and fully alive. So we slugged it out the first day. And it's gone really great since then. So the bottom-line learning for me is to be the radiant bitch that I am, and it all works out."

They both cracked up. Then Stella said, "Okay, Zeke-bear, your turn. Bottom-line learning for you?"

Zeke sat back and was quiet for a moment. "Let me see—well, I know this is going to come as a big shock to you, but some of my other co-leaders have suggested that perhaps I take up too much space in the room."

Stella said, smiling, "No—I can't imagine that!"

Zeke said, "Yes, it's true! Anyway, I used to ascribe it to my passion and my enthusiasm. It wasn't my problem. I just needed my co-leader to step up and play as big as I was playing.

"But with the Unicorns, I discovered that sometimes it comes from my not trusting my co-leader. In the second retreat, I just didn't have it in me to play so big. I was a little scared that the whole thing would come tumbling down. But it didn't. And in the third retreat, you nailed me on my garbage. You were every bit as big as I was, and each time the whole thing went off seamlessly. So those were two places where I saw that there was still more stuff I needed to learn about how to lean in.

"It's definitely not about playing small so someone else can play big. But I learned how to lean on you and let myself rely on you because I had to. I learned how to do that powerfully, just as powerfully as when I was supporting other people leaning on me."

Stella said, "You know, I'm sort of beginning to like leading with Eccentric types."

Zeke answered, "Hey, you know I'm all those types and much, much more!"

Then Stella hugged him and said, "Yes, you are. And I can't wait to lead with you again!"

Zeke kissed her forehead. "Me too!"

Emily had pulled over at a rest stop along I-5. She wanted to call Victoria to thank her for suggesting this whole leadership adventure. It was so much more amazing than a trip to Italy could ever be. The message on Victoria's voice mail said that she was back in the Congo and wasn't expecting to return for another two weeks. Emily got out of her car and stretched. As she watched the cars and trucks hurtling past, each on its own very important journey, she allowed herself to stand outside this stream of activity and energy for a moment.

She thought, *It really is up to me, isn't it? No one out there on that freeway knows or cares that I'm standing here watching them flying down the road. It won't matter to them if I live a little life or a big one. Only to me. And for me, I am getting tired of helping one person at a time. Just for myself, I want to touch the lives of as many teenage, insecure, self-hating girls as I can, and let them know that they are beautiful.*

Phil decided to swing by his office on his way home to let his staff know that he was going to take a couple extra days off, just to hang with his wife and his baby daughter. He drove into his company's parking lot and headed for his usual slot. The little sign read **Reserved for Phil Serrito**. He sat in his car, looking at the neat printing. That sign was going to have to go. There was always plenty of room in the parking lot, and a little walk couldn't hurt him. Actually, parking down at the end of the lot would give him a chance to chat at random with some of the people who worked there as they walked to their offices. Nope, this cherry parking spot was going to the employee of the month, not to him.

"So, what do you want to do on your first night home?" Violet reached across the table and took Isabel's hands in hers.

Isabel froze for an instant. She heard the panicked response inside her say, *What does that mean? Violet wants to do something. Come on, think of something! She is young and she wants some excitement. Francine is having a party. I bet Violet wants to go.*

Then Isabel took a breath, relaxed, and felt some space open up inside her. She chuckled. "Honey, all I want to do is start a fire, sit on the couch next to you, and listen to Rachmaninoff. Or maybe just listen to the evening."

Violet smiled. "Sounds delicious!"

Allen sat in the slightly uncomfortable, high-backed chair in front of the bishop's desk. He remembered those warm armchair chats he used to have with his last bishop, who was probably not coming back to take over his old position. Whatever Allen wanted, he was going to have to get from the dour man sitting behind this desk.

The provisional bishop said, "I have read your letter to be reassigned to a parish. And I also have the recommendation from your former bishop. Is there anything else you would like to say?"

Allen took a deep breath and imagined his Unicorn Tribe standing behind him, confidently on belay as he ascended this challenge. He began. "You don't have an easy job, do you? The last thing you need is scandal, and at one time I brought a breath of that to our church. I erred and misused my position, and I have atoned daily since then for my poor judgment. I lost my marriage and almost lost my cherished relationship with my daughter, who means the world to me.

"It was generous for the church to keep me in the fold and give me an administrative position to give me time to reflect on what I did. And now you have the difficult task of deciding whether or not I should go back into active ministry.

"I heard a song on the radio the other day, on a Christian rock and roll station. It was titled 'God's Not Finished with Me Yet.' I had to laugh. That is exactly how I feel. In a way, this devastating experience puts me in good stead as a minister. I have been humbled, and have seen firsthand how a good person can do ignorant and sinful things. I feel my calling very strongly, and I know I am ready to do the work of our church in an even more powerful manner because of this experience."

The provisional bishop tucked the papers in front of him back into a file folder and said, "Allen, I need to think on this. I will get back to you in a week."

Olivia sat in her favorite chair, gently stroking her cat's belly. "Ah, Magritte! Don't you dare scratch me! So I guess you're wondering where I have been the past week. Well, it's the last of those pesky retreats. Don't worry. I won't be deserting you anytime soon. You know, Mags, I have a lot more friends now, and I had some pretty amazing experiences. But all in all, I'm not quite sure if it was worth it."

Just then Magritte had had enough and went for her hand. She was ready for him and dumped him off her lap, laughing.

Chapter Ten

After It Was Over

Some believe there is nothing one man or one woman can do against the enormous array of the world's ills—against misery, against ignorance, or injustice and violence. Yet many of the world's great movements, of thought and action, have flowed from the work of a single man. A young monk began the Protestant Reformation, a young general extended an empire from Macedonia to the borders of the earth, and a young woman reclaimed the territory of France. It was a young Italian explorer who discovered the New World, and thirty-two-year-old Thomas Jefferson who proclaimed that all men are created equal. 'Give me a place to stand,' said Archimedes, 'and I will move the world.' These men moved the world, and so can we all.

Attributed to Robert F. Kennedy

O**livia sat** in the window, the afternoon sun warming her forearms. Her tabby cat lay on her lap, purring whenever she scratched under his chin. She was only partially listening to the phone call on her headset. She was still wondering if all the money and vacation time she had used up on Leadership was worth it. It had been six months since the program had ended, and not much had happened to improve her life. She was still teaching fifth grade, and it still felt like a dead-end job. She still didn't have a love interest. Life just felt grim, and there wasn't much she could do about it. And she was really getting sick of listening to Phil as he confronted Isabel on their monthly Unicorn Tribe call.

Phil was saying, "No, Isabel, it's not about going off and doing leadership with your board but then copping out in your relationship. Are you a leader only when you're getting paid? Does leadership happen only when you are sitting behind your desk? No way! If, like Stella said, a leader exists in each and every one of us human beings, why would we ever put that leader back in the closet? Especially when you're dealing with the woman you love!

"Look, leadership is a twenty-four-hour-a-day, seven-day-a-week commitment. It isn't parceled out in scattered moments over the course of a lifetime. It's a way of being in the world, an orientation to life and a way to be in relationship with others. Leadership is about you, Isabel, participating in and taking responsibility for everything that happens around you.

"You talked about being afraid to ask your partner to move in with you. Well, being a leader twenty-four-seven means we refuse to be victims of circumstance. We refuse to sit back and blame others for the state of our world. We are conscious and aware that with every breath, with every step, and with every word we speak, we are creating this universe and then dancing with all that the universe throws back to us. Dancing like Allen and Olivia did back in Retreat Three. You're not being willing to dance with her, and so you just end up blaming her for your unhappiness."

Emily chimed in, "I agree with Phil; it's twenty-four-seven. The other day, while I was standing in the checkout line at the grocery store, I decided to practice leadership. I realized that I had a choice as I was standing there. I could choose to be a 'line victim,' waiting impatiently or numbly zoned out, moving like a cow chewing my cud. I could leave the scene entirely and go into my head, to worry about what happened to me that morning or to plan that evening, while my body moved obediently forward. Or I could step out of that victim role, lift my head up, get present, choose a Stake, orient myself around it, and get into relationship with those around me from that Stake. So I decided to choose the Stake: 'Goodwill is a highly infectious virus, and I am a carrier.'

"The groceries were moving along the conveyor, past the scanner, and into the bags, as always. The carts were moving along the line and out the door, as always. Yet within minutes the atmosphere became completely different as a result of my leadership.

"And it wasn't just because I started to chat with the people around me. It truly became viral. Not only were people smiling at me, they started interacting with each other. Everyone started becoming a bit more present and connected. It was the coolest grocery line I had ever been in."

"Exactly," Allen added. "The only effort required of any of us is the choice to take a stand as a leader. It would have taken no more energy for Emily to move through that line like a cow than it did for her to move through as a leader. Yet I think we all have an old belief that it's harder to be a leader. I think it's just the opposite. I believe that we actually receive energy when we take leadership, especially in those situations where we would normally just be a cow and *mooove* on through."

Everyone laughed, even Olivia. But all through that day, she kept thinking about what Emily and Allen had said. That evening she broke from her normal routine of turning on a sitcom, grabbing her ceremonial one glass of brandy, and zoning out. Instead, she pulled out the journal that she had kept during her year in Leadership. She began to notice how very many times during that year she had written about how alive she felt.

What had happened to her? Had she just blindly returned to her old, slightly depressed life? These days, she felt like even more of a victim of her life than she had six months ago, when the leadership program had ended. She felt even more tired, burned out, and stressed out these days. The thought of being a leader at work, or even in the grocery line, made her feel exhausted. She realized that she had gone back to sleep and it sucked! She remembered that

Zeke had said something about leader burnout, and she went back through her journal until she found her notes about it. As she read them, she could hear his deep voice again in her imagination.

"Our opinion is that things like overwhelm and burnout happen for leaders when they lose connection with their Stake. It's very easy to be overwhelmed by the mad rush of particles, the fires to put out, the reactions, the judgments, and all the other things that are always flying around in the chaos that surrounds us. Without that Stake, we scurry from reaction to reaction, wearing ourselves out in the process.

"When you have a clear Leader's Stake, you can orient yourself to all of those whizzing particles and choose which to pay attention to and how they relate to what you are up to. You can get a feel for the timing of the things and the urges that arise in you in relationship to your Stake, and act on them. When you're orienting to your world through the lens of that Stake, you can slow things down and choose what to act on and what to ignore.

"When you're truly 'at choice' in your life, you're much less likely to be overwhelmed or to find yourself in a place of burnout. In fact, we can state with confidence that not only is Co-Active Leadership highly energizing and a way to live life twenty-four hours a day, seven days a week, it's the most effective antidote to leader burnout and overwhelm."

Olivia realized that she had no Stake. She had abandoned her Leader Quest the week after Leadership had ended. And week by week, she had systematically let go of everything she had learned over that year, sinking back into her gray comfort zone.

So where was she supposed to set a Stake in her life? She knew it was a bigger question than "What do I want?" What she wanted or needed had to do only with her own little ego. Stakes were about much bigger things. But where was she supposed to lead? She had seen some of the other Unicorns' Quests fade away because they were just good ideas, but not inspired by a passion so strong that nothing would stop them. Did she care about anything that much?

She could see how her whole life was built around the idea that if she never cared too much about any one thing, she would never be deeply disappointed. Yet that was actually a lie. She was deeply disappointed in her life right now, a life that she was living in a safe prison of not wanting anything.

Okay, she needed help. In the back of her journal was the phone contact sheet, and she saw that Stella lived in the same time zone as she did. She reached for her phone.

"Hello, Stella, this is Olivia Stimson. I was in the Unicorn—"

Stella interrupted, "Hello, Olivia, I recognized your voice. How are you?"

"Oh, uh, actually not very good. Do you have a minute to talk?"

Olivia could hear Stella's warm smile in her voice. "Sure, no problem. What's going on?"

"Well, life has been pretty crappy since Leadership ended, and I realized after listening to the tribe call this morning that I have been all messed up around this Quest thing. Everything I think of just seems too noble, too ambitious, and pretty soon I just get too scared to do anything at all."

Stella laughed. "Oh, baby, I am so with you. I totally failed for a year after I went through Leadership. I had all these grand ideas about becoming a political leader for Native Americans, empowering women and organizing social-action groups on the res. Everything I tried went bust. And I blamed everyone else around me. Finally I realized something: I hated organizing people to take political action. I was trying to do something I disliked, because the cause was just and the vision was grand. Didn't work worth a damn.

"That was when I asked myself, 'What do I like to do?' Well, I loved to play soccer. And then I asked myself, 'Who do I care about?' Well, I care about teenage girls on my reservation. Then it all came together. So I started a girls' soccer league, and I still coach the Lightning Hawks, the meanest, most kick-ass all-girl soccer team in northern Wisconsin. We took All State last year. And those girls are standing damn proud. You can change the world anywhere. It doesn't have to be in Washington, DC."

Olivia said, "That's the problem. I don't know what I really care about."

Stella said, "Okay, so, as I recall, you teach public school, right?"

Olivia answered, "Yep, fifth grade. I've been doing it for ten years, and it's getting pretty stale for me."

"Okay," Stella said, "that's a starting point. What got you into teaching in the first place?"

"My fifth-grade teacher, Mrs. Loper. She was a lifesaver for me."

"So, if Mrs. Loper were on the line right now, what would she tell you that would help you find a Stake around your career?"

Olivia sighed. She saw Mrs. Loper in front of her, with her black hair pulled back in a tight bun, her tall, wiry body leaning toward her, her intense blue eyes gleaming. Then Olivia smiled.

"She would say, 'It is time to stop thinking that the job of a teacher is to cram information down kids' throats. The most important things a teacher teaches her students are how to learn, how to care about each other, and how to live.' She certainly did that for me."

"Wow. Do I have someone you absolutely need to talk to, a graduate of one of the leadership programs CTI did in Europe. Hold on and I'll find her number for you."

Later that night, Olivia did the math. For her it was 11:00 PM, which would be 5:00 AM in Paris. She set her alarm for 4:00 AM and turned off the light.

It was very dark out when the alarm went off. She almost decided to hit the switch and go back to sleep. But then she thought about Mrs. Loper. *Okay, what the hell.* She started to dial.

Olivia was a little surprised at how eager Celeste Schenck was to talk to this total stranger. After all, she was the president of a university in France. But soon they were chatting like old friends. Then Olivia asked the big question: "How did you use what you learned in the leadership program to get where you ended up?"

Celeste answered, "It wasn't a straight line. Before Leadership, I walked down a lot of roads. I guess I've been an academic refugee since the eighties, living inside universities since I got my PhD at

Brown in comparative literature. Teaching at Barnard College and then later at the American University of Paris sharpened my beliefs about the goals of education. I believe that the goal of all learning is not to pack away more knowledge but to become more fully human. The function of a university is to grow souls.

"Since I became president of the American University of Paris, I've had the opportunity to implement these beliefs. Our way of teaching has moved from the traditional 'teacher as expert, student as passive learner' model to one where teachers are resources but the predominant learning comes from students learning from each other, fully engaged in the process of discovery.

"I first found out about CTI four years ago, when I heard about Co-Active coaching, and realized it was very much aligned with the way I taught my classes. I borrowed the Co-Active coaching book from a colleague in London. I wanted to take coaching classes, but they weren't being offered in Europe at that time. Then, several weeks later, I was in New York and I saw a brochure for CTI's Leadership Program. The first European leadership group was beginning in a week, so I signed up.

"I have to admit that I went into Leadership thinking I might learn a few new skills. I had no idea how it would call me forth. When I started Leadership, I was considering leaving the university. Between my second and third leadership retreats, the current president of the university left and the board started a search for a new president. I realized my Leadership Quest included becoming the next president. From that position, I would be able to answer the next big question: 'What kind of university do I want to build?'

"Transforming the educational system from the old, authoritarian model to one of active education was a long journey. We started with team teaching, having professors from two differing disciplines teaching material about the same subject—for instance, looking at food from anthropological and economic perspectives. But even with this breakthrough, the basic lecture-exam model stayed intact. My goal was to create working groups of students, mini-communities of people who were learning from each other. I also wanted the education to extend beyond the classroom and beyond strictly academic study. I wanted my students to start movements and nongovernmental organizations that would have an impact on the part of the world that they were studying. In these ventures, teachers would become guides, coaches, resources, and counselors, rather than authorities.

"Let me give you one example. In Bucharest, three thousand orphans wander homeless, living sometimes literally in sewers. These children, as young as five or six years old, live without any adult support or care, often needing to resort to prostitution to survive. A team of students from the university decided to make this situation into a project. In order to put this situation into context, they had to start by learning about the culture and history of Romania. They had to learn about sex trafficking, drug addiction, and economics. They studied business management before they could set up non-governmental organizations to serve these children.

"Of course, creating these projects produced entirely new headaches. How do you give a grade to a communal enterprise like this? How do you weigh the contributions of the individuals and the contribution of the group effort? These and many more were the kinds of challenges that innovators had to grapple with. There were many failures, and we slowly learned to celebrate the failures as necessary in any true change process. Fail magnificently. That is how we learn.

"Change came slowly. I was inaugurated as the president of the university the same week Barack Obama was inaugurated as the president of the United States. I've always felt a special sympathy with him, knowing how difficult it is to create real change from the top of the pyramid. Both of us faced real challenges from an economy in a recession. But those weren't our only obstacles.

"In the beginning, I often felt lost and alone, working in a system that was slow to change. It's rough going, shifting the status quo. I was faced with some tough decisions that left me feeling pretty isolated at first. Many old staff had to be replaced, and I discovered that a real leader has to have the capacity to carry a vision by herself when there is no one else to join her. And it's hard to be true to your dream when every day you feel like you are barely holding the boat together.

"At first, I tried doing it all by myself. That sure didn't work! I realized that I first needed to create a team I could trust and then delegate responsibilities to them. I needed someone to hold my rope and to be there for me when things got hot. I have that now, and it has made all the difference. My entire team took my vision and implemented it. Everyone is learning at the same time, and I really do mean everyone—the faculty, the students, the staff, and the trustees.

"We had to rebuild the entire governance structure of the school to pull this off. I don't think you can be an effective transformative leader until you have the team behind you to support the radical changes that you see need to be made.

"I hope to integrate some of the principles of Co-Activity and leadership that I learned at CTI throughout the university, perhaps even creating a leadership-like program for all my students. My Quest is like a never-ending road: there isn't a final destination, just a continually evolving challenge for all of us to become more flexible, more compassionate, more patient, more understanding, more human."

Something was stirring inside Olivia. When Celeste had said, "Everybody was learning," some half-formed idea had arisen within her. She had grown so sick of teaching to the tests.

She could start her class every day with a leadership circle. And what if all of her students created their own Leadership Quest, reporting back to the class how they had made their community a happier, friendlier, cleaner, and healthier place? What if everybody in her classroom was a leader? What would she have to create to make her room a place where curiosity reigned? What if she could get the whole school to become "more flexible, more compass- ionate, more patient, more understanding, more human?"

She had no idea what that meant, exactly, but for the first time in years, she was eager to get back to her classroom, just to discover what might be possible.

When the phone rang few minutes later, she thought it might be Celeste calling her back. But she was very wrong.

"Hi, Olivia, it's Allen."

"Allen, hi."

He cleared his throat. "Look, I just got some good news, and I wanted to tell somebody, so I thought of you. I am coming up to Westlake next Saturday to interview with a church up there. If they like me, I might finally get my dream: a congregation of my own. I checked it on Google maps—it looks like Westlake's pretty near where you live, right?"

She was happy for him. "Hey, congratulations! That is so great. I know how much you wanted to get out of administration. Yes, Westlake is just fifteen miles away. We will practically be next-door neighbors."

"So, Olivia, maybe we could get together Saturday night, if you're free."

"Sure, Allen, that would be fun."

Then came the shocker. "I really suck at this next part, but here goes—so, Olivia, we can get together as fellow Unicorns and chat about our lives, and that would be great. But what I would like even better would be if we got together for a date. Like, a real date—wine, a nice restaurant, that whole thing. I think about you a lot, and I'm wondering if you might be open to something like that."

Immediately, a list appeared in her mind, detailing why this was a terrible idea. *Play it safe. He's too old. He's out of shape. He's divorced and has a teenage daughter who would hate you. He plays around. He's too sentimental. He's still looking for a job. He's a minister, for God's sake!* The list went on and on.

What a crock! She laughed at herself. The guy was just asking her to go out on a date. It had been way too long since anyone had done that.

"Allen, this has been a very interesting morning already. I am discovering so many odd things about myself. And in answer to your question, yes, I think about you often, too. I would love to go on a date with you."

Some Final Thoughts from the Authors

To be a successful entrepreneur one needs a vision of greatness for one's work. If we dream extravagantly we will be inspired to forge a reality beyond the straight jacket of practicalities. There is a profound connection between art and enterprise which allows businesses to overcome the limitations of their existing visions.

Sir Ernest Hall

There is one last thing we need to say about leadership. We have talked about leadership twenty-four-seven and how to use the Leader's Stake as an antidote to burnout and overwhelm. But there is another phenomenon that is guaranteed to occur when you step out as the leader you were born to be. When you step out as a leader, you are stepping into unknown space. It is unknown to you and often unknown to most of those around you. When you step into this unknown space, it's pretty certain that the universe will have many surprises in store for you. These surprises can show up as unexpected successes, unplanned obstacles, unwelcome challenges, or the universe's just squatting and delivering all over your head.

Whatever the surprise, the key is to keep aligned with your Stake and keep stepping forward. It's not always easy or comfortable, and it won't always be fun. However, if you are connected to a Stake that is connected to your Life Purpose, we can guarantee that it will always be fulfilling and alive.

The most fundamental shift we see in the people who complete this program is that it becomes much more difficult for them stay asleep. Merely tolerating their world is no longer acceptable to them. They discover a compelling need to impact their world with their words and actions and, most importantly, with their intentions and choices.

We see people who were already "leaders" in their own worlds become more purposeful, powerful, and effective. We also see those leaders enjoying their lives more and taking more responsibility for themselves and the world around them. They come to abhor passing the buck or covering their butts.

We also see people who really never thought of themselves as leaders before step powerfully into living their life "on purpose." They surprise themselves and their world by showing up as leaders in situations where before there was little or no leadership.

We see people returning to their families as powerful leaders, taking responsibility for their impact and removing blame from their family system. We see leaders returning to their jobs with new purpose and a willingness to stand up for that purpose, sometimes believing they are risking too much, only to discover that their courage and conviction was exactly what was needed and wanted.

We see leaders who step forward with courage, even while they have no clear map or knowledge of how to transform a particular situation. But they step forward anyway, and keep stepping forward. Sometimes they fail and sometimes they succeed, but their purpose is never betrayed and their vision stays true. When they lead with an attitude of "I am going full steam ahead, no matter what," the universe throws challenges of every kind in their path. Yet they still stay true to their Stake and their Life Purpose.

Even when they are abandoned or unsupported, they stay aligned with their Stake as they move forward. They may reach their goals and achieve their outcomes, or they may achieve very different outcomes than they expected, sometimes even better ones than they expected. Then they make new goals and set down new outcomes to achieve, and they stay true. Whatever the outcome, they achieve a personal victory because they are pointing toward a purpose that is far greater than any one particular goal or outcome.

We invite you to use these Co-Active Leadership principles to become that kind of leader. And if these ideas excite you, we invite you to investigate the Leadership Program at CTI. The world needs your great leadership!

The Type System for Acting from Your Strength

Danger Type

The energetic impact of a Danger type on others is one of stillness, edginess, and discomfort. Think of the quality of the air just before a thunderstorm. There is electricity in the air, a sense of pending action, yet the air is very still. This is the impact of the Danger type. One often shifts in one's seat, feeling a little uncomfortable, in the presence of a Danger type. Telling the hard truth in a calm, matter-of-fact way, the Danger type helps us face what we sometimes fear. And while the Danger types' unswerving, icy-cool energy can sometimes be uncomfortable to be with, it also assures us that nothing will be avoided, so we get a sense of trust.

Sex Type

The energetic impact of a Sex type on others is one of physicality and movement. The Sex type makes others more aware of their own bodies and their physical sensations. When a Sex type is around, the temperature is hot. Their energy is often aggressive. It reaches out to you, and you may feel an urge to move your body, or, at a minimum, you will be much more aware of what you are experiencing within your own body. Sex types themselves are often moving their bodies, their arms, their hands.

Beauty Type

The Beauty type's energetic impact on others is reverence, depth, coolness, and stillness. Think of the placid surface of a pristine mountain lake: it's cool, clear, and inviting. But don't be diverted by the word itself. The Beauty type is not about being physically beautiful—it's about bringing a sense of deep appreciation for all things. In the presence of a Beauty type, we feel drawn in. We become aware of our emotions, often feeling moved by what the Beauty type is saying or doing. We feel a sense of grace, dignity, and divinity in the presence of a person who is on type as a Beauty.

Charm Type

The energetic impact of a Charm type is warmth and connection. When someone is fully expressed as a Charm type, we feel more at ease; we're relaxed and often prepared to have fun. Charm types are frequently able to be irreverent or tell the 'hard truth' in a casual, easy way, so that others can hear it without being offended. In the presence of a Charm type, we want to hang out, be connected, have a cup of coffee, and enjoy the world around us.

Humor Type

Follow the laughter, and you will probably find a Humor type. The energetic impact of a Humor type is lightness, but Humor types are not necessarily funny. However, they do a lot to shift the energy in a group from heaviness or consternation to ease and lightness. Humor types differ from Charm types because their impact on others is coolness and amusement, rather than the warmth and engagement of a Charm type. In a work situation, when a team gets stuck in a quagmire over a difficult issue and things are starting to feel grim, just like turning on a light in a dark room, the Humor type will say or do something that effortlessly shifts the energy to an easier, more fun-loving experience for everyone.

Eccentric Type

The energetic impact of an Eccentric type is angularity, unpredictability, and delight. Other descriptors of this type include quirkiness or twitchiness. Eccentric types often see the world in a very different, more unconventional way than the rest of us. Sometimes they move their bodies with a delightful awkwardness that's very compelling, despite its oddity. In the presence of an Eccentric type, non-Eccentrics often feel a bit on guard because they don't know what unexpected and strange thing will happen next. It is very interesting, and sometimes a bit disturbing, leading with one. Eccentric types help the rest of us appreciate the weirdness of things.

Intelligence Type

A place where all these types meet is the Intelligence type. The Intelligence type's energetic impact is smoothness, clarity, and competence. The strength of this type isn't about being intellectually smart; it is about conveying a sense of capability and often includes curiosity. When you are in the presence of an Intelligence type, the air feels clear. Even when an Intelligence type has no idea of the answer to a thorny question, those around him or her will feel they are in capable hands and the issue will be competently resolved. The energetic temperature around an Intelligence type is cool. There isn't much drama or emotional turmoil; instead, there's a sense of ease and stability.

Bibliography and References

Works Cited in the book

With so many versions of books, newspapers, and journals these days, including electronic publications, it becomes increasingly challenging to determine original, definitive sources that are readily accessible to the general public. So we have chosen to identify sources that can at least be identified in libraries and through on-line searches.

De La Fontaine, Jean. *Fables*, first published 1668.

Ruiz, Don Miguel. *The Four Agreements*. San Rafael, CA: Amber-Allen Publishing, 1997.

Rukeyser, Muriel. *The Speed of Darkness*. New York: Random House, 1968.

Williamson, Marianne. *A Return to Love: Reflections on the Principles of a Course in Miracles*. New York: Harper Paperbacks, 1992.

(Note: Marianne Williamson's quotation used in this book is often cited as having been used by Nelson Mandela at his presidential inauguration on May 9, 1994. President Mandela and Marianne Williamson have both repeatedly denied this.)

The poem "Lean In" is an original work by David Skibbins. He created it during a CTI Leadership Program.

Chapter Heading Quotations

The quotations at the start of each chapter are from various sources, some original, some from reliable collections of quotations. In some cases, the original source cannot be confirmed. It's the message that counts!

Introduction   Lance Secretan. *Industry Week*, October 12, 1998.

Chapter 1   Margaret Mead

Chapter 2   Ralph Waldo Emerson

Chapter 3   Harold Geneen

Chapter 4   John Quincy Adams

Chapter 5   Eleanor Roosevelt. *You Learn by Living*. Louisville, KY: Westminster John Knox Press, 1960.

Chapter 6   Napoleon Bonaparte

Chapter 7   Attributed to Goethe

Chapter 8   Wangari Maathai. Nobel Lecture. December 10, 2004.

Chapter 9   Harry Truman

Chapter 10   Attributed to Robert F. Kennedy, contained in the press release of the eulogy delivered by Senator Edward M. Kennedy, June 8, 1968.

Epilogue   Sir Ernest Hall

Acknowledgments

Without Karen Kimsey-House and Laura Whitworth this book would not have happened. They worked with Henry since 1989 co-creating, co-designing, co-leading, and co-founding CTI and all of its programs, including the Leadership Program. We miss Laura, who passed away in 2007, who brought so much passion and commitment, not to mention the fountain of ideas to this work.

We want to acknowledge all the faculty and alumni of the Co-Active Leadership Program. These amazing people are taking a stand every day of their lives for growing human consciousness and responsibility. They believe that every human being has a purpose and is committed to making a difference with their lives.

We want to thank Victoria Bentley, Celeste Schenck, and Ted van der Put for sharing their stories and allowing us to include them in our book, and mostly for what they are doing for this world.

We want to thank all those who read the manuscripts and gave us insights and feedback and helped us shape this journey.

We want to thank the editing team—Claire Robson, John Breeze (a Waterdragon), Brooke Warner, and Barrett Briske.

Most of all we want to thank the co-leaders of our lives, Karen and Marla. They put up with a lot of nonsense so that we can do what we do. We love you.

Author Bios

Henry Kimsey-House, CPCC, MCC

Co-founder and Director, CTI

One of the first professional coaches in the 1980s, Kimsey-House is the co-founder and lead designer of CTI's thought-provoking, experiential learning programs and the co-author of Co-Active Coaching, the best-selling industry coaching bible, now in its third edition.

An actor since age nine, Kimsey-House honed his insights into human emotion and the narrative process through classical theatrical training and years of stage, television, and film experience.

With deep conviction that education should be driven by immersive, contextually based learning and not dry information dumps, Kimsey-House is committed to creating richly engaging and transformative learning environments where retention approaches 80 percent, rather than the traditional 20 percent. He continues to develop new, innovative curricula in collaboration with other dynamic thought leaders. He lives with his wife, Karen Kimsey-House, on the coast of Northern California.

David Skibbins, PhD

David Skibbins works as a life coach with entrepreneurs, business owners, other coaches, and upper level managers.

A coach supervisor at CTI, he is certified by the ICF as a Professional Certified Coach. He has a PhD in clinical psychology and was a psychotherapist for over twenty years.

He is the author of *Becoming a Life Coach: A Complete Workbook for Therapists*; *Working Clean and Sober*; and *The Tarot Card Murders*, a four-book, award-winning murder-mystery series published by St. Martin's Press.

David is also a playwright, an actor, and a director in several local theater groups on the North Coast of California.